Daddy's Baby, Mama's Maybe

Daddy's Baby, Mama's Maybe

I Am Not My Conception

COME LAMORE

Copyright © 2020

All rights reserved. No part of this book may be reproduced in any written, electronic, recording, or photocopying without written permission of the publisher or author. The exception would be in the case of brief quotations embodied on the pages where the publisher or author specifically grants permission.

Books may be purchased in quantity and/or special sales by contacting the author.

Published by
Mynd Matters Publishing
715 Peachtree Street NE, Suites 100 & 200
Atlanta, GA 30308
www.myndmatterspublishing.com

978-1-953307-23-1 (Paperback)
978-1-953307-24-8 (Hardcover)
978-1-953307-25-5 (eBook)

FIRST EDITION

To my mother and anyone who has been a victim of sexual assault, the product of sexual assault, and anyone who has committed sexual assault and needs to know the effect it has on all involved:

I pray that any woman and/or man who is aware of any type of paternity secrets will stand up and speak out! This is far too common and goes on much more than people know. Children have the right to know where they come from, who they belong to, and how they got here. There is nothing more hurtful than being mistreated and verbally abused by loved ones about something you had absolutely nothing to do with.

A child does not determine their DNA. A child does not determine who the father is and the only way a woman should do so is to sleep with exactly who you want that father to be and only him. If you did not, the decision is no longer yours. Be honest and work it out. Even if you don't want to be with the father, he has a right to know he is the father and do with the information what he chooses to. You have enough in you to love that child regardless of the circumstances and if you feel you don't, please reach out to someone who will.

"There's no way I can pay you back, but my plan is to show you that I understand. You are appreciated!"
-Tupac Shakur

CONTENTS

LIKE LOVE, LIKE LOVE..................................9

AFTER THE LOVE IS GONE 15

TOO BLIND TO SEE.......................................23

CABBAGE PATCH 27

DADDY'S HOME..31

THE BIRDS AND THE BEES 35

CHANGE GONNA COME..............................39

THANKS FOR MY CHILD 45

STORM IS PASSING OVER............................51

DOUBLE OR NOTHING 55

THREE'S COMPANY.......................................59

BLACK BUTTERFLY..65

STING LIKE A BEE 67

SUNSHINE AFTER THE RAIN 79

PROMISE TO LOVE 83

LIFE IMITATES ART 89

MIRROR IMAGE 97

LOVE DON'T LIVE HERE ANYMORE 101

LOVE IS A HOUSE	111
OLD HABITS DIE HARD	115
IRISH TWINS	125
IF YOU LOVE THEM, SET THEM FREE	129
CELEBRATIONS, GRADUATIONS, SALUTATIONS	143
SHIT HIT THE FAN	151
THIS YEAR I RESOLVE TO	155
IF IT ISN'T LOVE	169
GRACE AND MERCY COVERED ME	183
IF I COULD	187

LIKE LOVE, LIKE LOVE

I was born in 1974 on a Texas army base to parents, Mick and Sherie. At least that's what I believed to be true for most of my life.

As a child, I remember hearing kids being called bastards and always being proud of the fact that I was not deemed, *illegitimate*. My parents were married when I was born, my daddy wanted a baby, and I was the gift he got the day after his birthday. What could be better?

When my parents met, my father had no children and my mother had a daughter, my older sister Regina. Mama got pregnant at fifteen with Regina by an older man. It was said that my grandmother ran him out of town threatening to have him arrested for statutory rape. As a result, my sister never met her father. Ever.

My mother came from a family of thirteen and

landed somewhere in the middle. Her parents had a complex marriage which included a few children being born by different men. Because my grandfather was a man of honor and family structure, he raised the children as his own until the day he died. Both of my grandparents drank when they were young so their relationship had some rough spots. My grandmother, Katherine, was a force to be reckoned with. She was neither meek nor mild but if you brought it, she would definitely finish it. Therefore, it was always best to mind yours and stay out of hers. The grandfather I knew, CL, was quiet and fun. He had his moments when he was drinking, but I only witnessed the fun side of him even then. My mother was described as a whiney poo poo who cried all the time as a child and just couldn't be given enough love. She was not considered a "problem" child though so everyone was surprised when she showed up pregnant. She was hanging out with the wrong crowd and got caught up in the madness. *This would eventually resurface in her adult life.*

My daddy was the oldest of ten kids, including two sets of twins. My grandfather drank but my grandmother did not. She was a quiet, obedient wife who did as she was told. They were not together when I was a child so I don't have many details of their marriage. Daddy witnessed his younger brother's death as a teenager and eventually left home behind it. The details are very sketchy and he has never mentioned any of it to me. I was told by a cousin when I was nine and as you could imagine, I was in disbelief. None of my father's relatives would tell me anything so I asked my mother's sister, aunt Trish, and she told me what she knew. It was a tragic incident and unfortunately, he never got the emotional and psychological help he needed and would pay for it for the rest of his life.

Enough history, now back to me…

So, my parents met and my daddy was very quickly smitten with my mother and adored her young daughter and decided he wanted to marry her. He joined the U.S. Army as a means to support his future family. My mother always told me she did not love him and only married him to get out of washing dishes at home. After all is said and done, I'm sure she was telling the truth.

They got married and he was sent to Texas for basic training where my mother and sister joined him. Once they got settled in, my mother immediately felt the emotional strain of being away from her family.

Plus, my daddy was drinking and fighting her. She said he would wake up out of his sleep and attack her if he had been having a nightmare. He would often cry out his brother's name in his sleep too. She started visiting her family back home in Louisville just to get away.

Upon returning from one of her visits, she realized she was pregnant. My sister was two at the time and Daddy was delighted to hear they were expecting another child. His attitude changed somewhat because he was finally going to have a child of his own to love and cherish. But one night when she went into the kitchen and cut on the light, he dove off of the counter and onto her. His behavior was taking a toll on her and my sister and she knew it wouldn't be much longer before she left. He said all he ever wanted was a baby girl. That really shocked me because I thought all men wanted a son first. Nope, not my daddy. He only wanted a girl and that's what he got. I was his only daughter too. Even considering his many romantic trysts, he never had anymore.

The day after his birthday in 1974, I was born. My daddy named me after his favorite Bobby Womack song at the time, *Come L'amore*. The song meant, "like love" in Spanish. My aunts always told me stories about how happy and proud he was when I was born. He sang to me and showed me off to everyone. They said he had one of the cutest chocolate babies they had ever seen. All of this sounded really corny to me then, but it wasn't until my aunt Bea played the song for me at twelve and I heard the lyrics, that I truly felt the sincerity of it all. Tears welled in my eyes as I listened. I don't know if he was singing about his child or the woman he loved but it was so sweet. My heart filled with pride to know that someone loved me as much as this man loved whoever he was singing about.

AFTER THE LOVE IS GONE
1976

By the time I turned two, my parents were divorced. I don't know too much about the specifics, but I know my mama left him and he ended his career in the Army trying to follow her. She has been known to give second chances, but I think in light of the fact she never loved him anyway and that he abused her, she was done with him. She went back to Louisville and prepared to raise her two girls.

When she returned home, she did not have a plan for survival and very quickly started associating with the wrong people, which was not good for our family. She started using drugs, running the streets, and leaving us with her sisters and parents whenever she could. By the time I was three, Aunt Peg became fed up with her and moved me and my sister to live with her in Vista, California for three months. I graduated from preschool there and had some really happy times. While in California, Aunt Peg was told that I was gifted and needed to be surrounded by educational opportunity. After we got back to Kentucky, I began head-start. I excelled in everything I attempted and was skipped to the first grade the next year. School quickly became a safe haven for me. I was popular, smart, and able to choose activities that made me happy.

For some reason, we were moving every year when I got back with my mother. My father moved to Illinois shortly after the divorce and during those years, I really don't remember him being involved in my life. I recall being about five or so and his family taking me to Illinois to see him. I had fun visiting with him but at that age, I still preferred my mom and was ready to come back home.

My mother got to the point where she only had men around who could give her money for her habit and her children. She was turning tricks, stripping, and boosting for money. We were always dressed nicely and lived in nice surroundings, but she was disappearing more and more for longer periods of time. Our family began to worry about her lifestyle and how it would affect us.

While in the first grade, I lost one of the early male figures in my life. My youngest uncle, Patrice, died under suspicious circumstances and I was terribly sad. He was fun, wild, and spoiled me rotten. I spent a great deal of time with Patrice but didn't realize until he was gone that he had major issues. There was some controversy that went on while he was alive, but being a kid, I missed it. Also during that time, a male family member was accused of molesting young girls and teens in my family. I later learned, I had been bribed with gifts and goodies as he molested some of them. To this day, I do not know why he never bothered me but it may have had something to do with the fact that I had a really big mouth.

During the summer after first grade, my mother left us home in the care of an aunt. No clue where she was or which aunt it happened to be, but I remember that Regina told me to go to the store and put some air in the tires on her ten speed. Off I went to the store to get the air because she was more of a guardian to me by this point than anyone else and I knew to obey her. On my journey, I failed to look both ways and was hit by a car. I blacked out for a minute but I remember hearing people yelling and crying and being loaded into the ambulance. Someone found my aunt and she made her way to the site of the accident. My mother was MIA until later that night. She came to the hospital with an entourage and didn't even stay the night with me. I remember waking up to see the mother of the young man who hit me. She brought me toys and goodies and apologized for my pain. I didn't see my mother much during my hospital stay but was released into her care. We were able to sue the family and received a settlement. The money would prove to be more of a curse than a blessing.

I wasn't home long before she started leaving again. My aunt Peg and uncle Tee picked me up and I spent the remainder of the summer at their house. I felt like a princess. Tee carried me from room to room and they pampered me every day of my vacation and he had a cute son there I liked who would later become my husband in a child mock wedding! But when school started back up, I had to go back home.

I started the second grade on crutches and wasn't really happy to go to school at all. The teachers knew what to expect when I got there and helped make the transition easier for me. My mother got a new boyfriend and we learned we would be moving. Lucky me, I was going to change schools…again.

There were a lot of ups and downs during this period, but I also remember having a lot of fun. My mother was either out late at night or entertaining customers during the day so my sister and I had the run of the place. We played outside and in our friends' houses.

Before I knew it, summer had come and gone, and we were moving again. As I entered third grade, school was more enjoyable because I had a boyfriend named Lee. Up until about the age of twelve, Lee was the love of my life. We played in the park together every day after school. During school, we were not such a public couple, but at home I knew he was *the one* as did he. Lee had beautiful skin, curly hair, and was tall and skinny. He was a bit of a crybaby, but I enjoyed being there to comfort him when the other boys picked on him. I guess he kind of set the mold for the desire in me as a woman to date men with curly hair.

We lived at several different places during that year. I may have changed schools two or three times. At some point, we shared my grandmother's house with my uncle and his family. Both he and my mother ran the streets while his girlfriend, Chan, took care of us. I was relatively happy there, but Chan was a depressed woman due to my uncle doing everything under the sun right in her face, so we had to make our own fun. And we did. We played school, house, and whatever else our imagination led us to do. Somewhere around this time, my sister met her brother Joe. We just happened to be walking home from the park one day and some adult on our porch called the kids walking with us to come over. When my mother came out, she recognized him and told my sister that he was her brother. We stared at her, wondering if she was high or simply out of her mind. He looked nothing like my sister, no one had ever so much as hinted a word about a brother, and we played together every day in the park. Nevertheless, he was her father's son. Apparently, his mother did not want him to know either because he was just as shocked as we were. He started to come around and hang out with us behind his mother's back because she did not respond too kindly to the introduction. When he came to visit, Regina would ask him about their father. He told her that their father called on certain days of the week and he would try to give him our number so she could speak with him. That call never came. He eventually faded away and life went on.

My mama and Chan ended up having some sort of spat, so we moved out. We went to some old man's house in the projects where she said we'd stay a few nights. I remember the tears rolling because I didn't want to leave, change schools, or stay at a stranger's creepy apartment. He had plastic on his antique couches and that is where I had to sleep. It smelled of cigarettes and mildew and I guess that's where I get some of the feelings I have now. I didn't sleep that night and anxiously awaited daylight so I could head to school.

But it kept getting worse. After we left his house, we went to stay with a female friend of hers in the same projects. She had two little girls who we loved to play with. The problem was, both mothers were on drugs, so we were alone a lot. Shelly, the lady next door, had two sons, Rich and Ace, who also played with us. Ace was a skinny, dark boy with a gorgeous smile. He liked me and I knew it but I still had eyes for Lee and no one else. As I got older, I put two and two together to realize that the older boy was molesting the daughter of the lady we were staying with. There was an occurrence of sexual games being played and it was bordering on incest and molestation. I think most of it was kids emulating things they had seen adults doing at home and/or on TV. Most of the time, I was the lookout person because I talked a lot and would be more likely to tell if I saw too much. There were times though that I participated. I can safely say, to my knowledge, there was no penetration.

TOO BLIND TO SEE
1983

My mother started dating Rudy, a blind man around the corner from where we were staying. He seemed nice and quickly hit it off with us. His home was clean, comfortable, and smelled good. Contrary to being blind, he could cook really well. I wasn't happy about possibly changing schools again but if I had to live anywhere, his place was a good place to be.

Things went well in the beginning, but it wasn't long before my mother started leaving to get high against Rudy's wishes. In spite of their problems, they got married. I was angry because it didn't feel right. It had to be for money because we hadn't known him long. However, I had to grin and bear it because no one listens to children.

I had to change schools again and was very upset this time. By now, my friends started asking me why we moved so much. I was at the age where these sorts of things could label you. I complained as often as I could, but my mother was no longer in the "sorry" mood. She was mean and grumpy and started threatening to hit us when we got out of line. Life got really crappy but I had nowhere to go. My father was practically unheard of during this time and I wasn't spending as much time with his family anymore. I think it's safe to say that everyone in my life was going through it for different reasons. Some of them were abusing alcohol and drugs or being abused by men and that took precedence over raising kids.

My mother and her husband began to argue and fight incessantly. I can recall one incident in particular where Rudy was chasing my mother around the apartment. How exactly does a blind man do that? To this day, I am still amazed. I saw him drive a car too. But any who, he had her in a corner and somehow, she got away. She ran into the kitchen to hide, and he went straight to where she was. We then hid behind a couch in the living room. He came there too. Maybe he found us because his apartment was so small and he knew every inch of it by heart. After that incident, we left and moved into our own apartment. I was glad to leave even though I liked Rudy. I stayed in touch with him over the years and even attended his funeral when he passed away in 2008.

We hadn't had a place of our own in so long, so having one felt good. We moved to public housing which was a small upgrade from where we were. I wasn't so worried about schools this time and was looking forward to meeting new people.

I started fourth grade at yet another new school. We moved into one of the better income-based apartments over the summer, so I had plenty of time to make friends before school year started. That was always my strong suit, so I had many when school began. In spite of all of the chaos I had experienced, I felt really good about the move. We hadn't had an apartment of our own in a long time. We also moved near the complex Rudy lived in so I still could see some of the same people.

Regina was approaching her teens and becoming more rebellious, giving mama a run for her money. Around this time is when they had their first fist fight. Mama yelled at her for breaking curfew and she said something back. When mama hit her for doing so, she balled up her fist and hit her back. It was awful. We had a house full of people and it took everyone to separate them. I knew the tide would turn when she was allowed to stay there that night. She figured she was mama's equal at that point and things would get so much worse for me.

For whatever reason, my daddy started to call and send letters again. Maybe my mama cut off contact while we lived with Rudy or something. I learned at this time that he was incarcerated. The news didn't hit me as hard because it was time for him to come home and he kept in contact so well, I never knew the difference. Plus, I just loved my daddy.

CABBAGE PATCH
1984

My paternal aunt and grandmother came to get me more because word on the street was that my mother was abusing drugs more often and we were being left at home alone or with an old man a lot. That old man was the latest conquest. His name was Edward. I don't know exactly how mama met him, but he was old. Think…gray hair, glasses, and fake teeth old.

Edward was the sweetest thing though. He had a really good job, so he paid the bills for mama and bought us pretty much whatever we asked for. He had a sweet tooth too so the two of us really hit it off. He always came home from his work with plenty of candy for us to share.

During the relationship, mama learned she was pregnant. Regina and I were both excited because we wanted a brother. We were old enough to help care for the baby and figured it may slow mama down some. The only thing was, mama still had a few other guys she dealt with so we didn't know exactly who the baby's daddy would be. We didn't care. Mama started going to church while she was pregnant, and the church even had a baby-shower for her. Things were looking pretty good. I was proud to learn that I was going to be a big sister. I planned to be a good big sister and not bully and torture the baby as my sister had done to me for most of my life.

Much to our surprise, the baby brother we were waiting for turned out to be a baby sister! We kept her though because she was a big, chunky, chocolate Cabbage Patch doll! She had a head full of curly black hair and the biggest cheeks and thighs. Mama named her after my aunt Peg, and everyone was delighted to meet our little doll. Shortly after giving birth, mama got her tubes tied and was back into the streets the same week. I looked after the baby most of the time because Regina was out with her friends and Edward was old and had some sort of sleeping disorder where he fell asleep as soon as he sat down. My new sister spent most of her days and nights with me. She was born in the summer, so I had all the time in the world to love on her. At one point, she got pneumonia and had to be hospitalized. I just cried and cried worrying that my baby was not going to make it. Thankfully, she made it through and came back home better than ever.

As the summer neared its end, mama and Edward started having public fights. My dad's sister came and got me when she heard what was happening. The last weekend, Edward shot a gun into the window because he thought my mama had another man in the apartment. I only heard about the story though because I wasn't home when it happened. My oldest aunt owned a duplex, so she let us move in with her. I was entering middle school and had to change schools yet again. I was sad though because I had some really cool friends where we lived. I even had a boyfriend. He was older than me and kissed me on the lips. Hanging out with my sister as a spy began to put me in older situations that my body wasn't ready for. She would often make me participate in the kissing and clothes burning sessions or threaten to say I did even if I didn't. Mama was out a lot so we had boys over whenever she was gone.

DADDY'S HOME
1986

My daddy moved back to Louisville about this time with his girlfriend and her daughter who was the same age as me. I would visit them on the weekends but soon realized it was not a good idea. My dad and his girlfriend would get into violent arguments that led to physical eruptions. He would drink several beers and go off when she said the slightest thing to me. He was very protective of his daughter. She wasn't really mean to me, but I think she felt some kind of way about me because she could tell my daddy was still crazy about my mama.

Regardless, her daughter and I hit it off. She ended up at the same middle school I attended and I welcomed her into my social circle so we could hang out all the time. We both realized we could do without each other's parent in our lives. She actually started staying at my house more often. Everybody loved being there because my mother was a riot when she was home. She let us be teens and had fun watching us do so.

My older sister was in and out and doing her own thing. She started joining gangs, experimenting with street drugs, and was very rebellious. Mama was not on drugs anymore and thus the battle began. I guess we kind of acted out worse because we were able to do what we wanted for so long and we felt like she was being all phony and sanctified now. She'd started going to church and made us go several days a week.

Somewhere down the line, she hooked up with this drunkard who eventually led her back into the streets. After a few months of the usual, she went into rehab yet again and we went to stay with my grandmother and grandfather. This time was tough because we had our friends near home who we wanted to hang out with. Lucky for me, my grandparents lived just up the road from my daddy's family, so I had an outlet.

Regina started kicking it with us and eventually she met a guy she really liked. They started hanging out a lot and I had a boyfriend I really felt special about too. It was hard living with the grandparents because they were not as lenient as mama. We found a way around it though. At least we didn't have to change schools. I was in my second year of middle school, had several good friends, and bonds being built. Even though mama was in the hospital, we were happy.

When she got out, we went back home. Although she wasn't on drugs, she wasn't home either. She was dating and staying out with the chosen beau most nights. My sister was still dating Gene, the fifteen-year-old boy she met while we lived with grandma. Right after her sixteenth birthday, she got pregnant. I was excited about having a new baby around. Gene and I were pretty close being that I knew him first and introduced him to my sister.

As the pregnancy progressed, Regina and mama fought and argued. My sister was MEAN! I got tired of the noise. We argued too but I knew how to get away from her before she attacked. However, there was one evening when only the two of us were home. We started arguing about something and it got really heated. She found Edward's gun and put it to my head telling me she would kill me if I kept talking. I didn't know if it was loaded or not but didn't care. I was tired of her and mama double teaming me and calling me names. When mama was home, they'd verbally assault me for telling other family members things they would do. It got a little better when mama was in a relationship and my sister got more involved with her baby's father. I stood up to her physically that year and that would be the last time she actually put her hands on me.

THE BIRDS AND THE BEES
1988

We moved out of my aunt's duplex and into an apartment on the other side of town. I met a new set of friends and started dating an older guy named Lando. This relationship was more intense than my first few. Mama was still sober, but again, dating outside of the home so I got away with a little more. It wasn't long before Regina told on me and the war began between me and my mother. She told the guy to stay away from me and made it clear I was not to go near him. He was seventeen and I was fourteen. Not too much of an age gap but there were some things he was into doing that someone my age just shouldn't do.

He drank and got high daily so she knew he would probably be damaging to my character. She got wind of the fact that we were having unprotected sex (also from Regina) and went off! She made me go to the doctor to be tested for pregnancy and STDs and immediately put me on birth control pills. Even though it was utterly humiliating, I continued to sneak around with him.

My sister and mother had a huge fight while she was pregnant, and I worried if any of us would survive it. I couldn't believe they would risk the baby's safety by fighting. She put her out as she often would, and the cycle continued.

Regina had my first nephew in 1988. I loved him with all of my heart. At first, he was premature and tiny. She continued to be mean and wouldn't even let me hold him. I had to sneak when she was in the shower or sleeping. We were all crammed in a two-bedroom apartment so things heated up. Regina and her boyfriend started fighting because he was out with other girls. She waited to hear of an affair and pounced on him and whoever the fool was caught with him. Mama started fussing at her about her unsavory behavior as a new mom thus igniting the next war between them. She would pack up the baby and storm out whenever mama said something she didn't like. I wasn't able to see him as much anymore and that hurt but I was glad to have her gone so we could have some peace in the house. I still looked after my little sister who just quietly sat and watched TV all day.

In 1988, I also met my stepsister Capri when mom dated her dad. She came to stay with us over spring break one year and we hit it off. She was a lot like my sister Regina but not jealous of me, so we got along wonderfully. She was just the big sister I needed. We kept secrets, talked all the time, and I even planned to visit her in Michigan. When my mom and her dad broke up though, we lost touch for many years.

Once Regina got her own place, I was able to visit and get away from mama, who started to watch me more closely once Regina was gone. I was drinking heavily, smoking marijuana, and having lots of sex with my older boyfriend. It wasn't that I really wanted to, but I went along with the flow. Once mama found out I was still seeing him, she started the proceedings to put me into a girl's home. She filed charges against him in court which prompted his mother to forbid him from having me in her house.

My daddy came to my rescue and took me to his house in lieu of me going to the girl's home. I was excited. He had a new girlfriend named Sheree who was pretty cool. I was uncomfortable with her when I first met her because she was white, and I had never experienced my daddy with anything other than

Black women. She seemed awkward with me too. It wasn't long though before we hit it off because she had a heart of pure gold. We watched TV together and listened to Anita Baker while my daddy was at work. He would come in late at night smelling of beer and talking loudly. I felt sorry for her because he was mean to her. Still, she put up with him for a long time.

I was still doing what I wanted and would see my boyfriend after school before I'd go back to my dad's place. Daddy let me know he knew what I was doing. Because he was intimidated by mama, the only thing he did was warn me to be sure she didn't see me when I was out her way. I secretly wished he would've had more backbone and told me to leave the guy alone. By that point, I was tired of him anyway, but he was like a stalker and would not let me go. I got tired of my daddy mistreating Sheree and the dysfunctional things taking place at his place so I eventually packed up and went back home.

CHANGE GONNA COME
1989

Mama started dating a man who lived in the complex named Nate. We ended up moving away from the complex into another apartment because he had children and we were getting cramped.

I was happy to get away. Lando went to jail, and that got him away from me (or so I thought). We moved into a new school district so my second year of high school was at another school. By now I had picked up several new friends, but I still hung out mostly with my best friend, Karm, who lived in the West End. We started going to concerts together, skating, and hanging out at the park. We were eleven when we met in middle school but now we were fifteen.

I rode the bus to Karm's house and stayed with her and her mother. It was funny because I finally got to see how my friends viewed my mother. Karm's mom was a blast! Whenever I stayed, we would team up on Karm and make her so mad. We both had really silly senses of humor, but they were alike. Karm was really funny too, but she had her own sense of humor. She didn't find our jokes about her boyfriend funny at all. I hated when it was time to go back home. Ms. Lee always let me know I was welcome anytime.

When I started the tenth grade, I wasn't really dating at all. I was getting used to the new school and the new people. I talked on the phone to guys but tried to get back into my studies because my ninth-grade year was horrible. I was no longer drinking and smoking so my head was clear. Mama married Nate before we moved from the apartments. Honestly, I wasn't thrilled about it. It was weird. I loved him when I went to his house to visit his daughter Tammie, but just couldn't sync with him dating my mother. He was a great guy though. He easily assimilated into his role as stepdad.

My daddy was in and out at this time, so it was appreciated. Nate taught me how to drive, change a tire, and bought me my first car. He was so giving and patient with all of us. His oldest daughter was a few months older than me and hell on wheels. She continued to fight the marriage, but I gave up after a few months and more threats of homelessness.

Some kind of way, Lando got our new address and slipped a note under our door. I was shocked to find it and relieved my mama didn't. The letter was really crazy. He was talking about how much he loved me, how he cried every night in jail thinking of me, and didn't want to live without me. I wrote him back letting him know that I didn't want ANYTHING to do with him. I explained that my life with him was too intense for me at that age and I was in a better place. He obviously understood and backed off.

After a year in our larger apartment, we moved into a house which was cool. I wasn't home much anyway so location was not an issue at all. I began the cycle of working every summer so I was always meeting new people to hang out with. I was labeled a social butterfly early on and it was definitely true. I wasn't the type to go around meeting someone new and quickly labeling them my friend. I honestly built lasting relationships and still communicate with many of them now.

While living in that house, I would graduate from high school, experience my mother's cancer, and become pregnant with my first child. Things were pretty good, but mom relapsed a time or two while we were there. Her marriage was tumultuous due to addiction, infidelity, and the strain of her declining health.

While getting documents together for my driver's test, I noticed that my middle name was different from what showed on my birth certificate. When I asked my mother about it, she simply said she didn't know. Told me to ask my daddy since he named me. She told me that after she gave birth, she made him take care of me. When I asked why she had none of my official documents, she again told me to ask my daddy for them. He told me how to call Texas and retrieve them.

One night in 1990, the phone rang. I answered it and it was my daddy. I could tell he had been drinking and he asked where my mother was. I told him she was asleep (there was an unwritten rule that she is never to be awakened from her sleep for phone calls) and he told me to wake her up. I hesitated but did it anyway because he sounded strange. She joined the call from her room and I held on to the phone to see what was going on.

He asked her what this news was about someone else being my father. She immediately started cursing him out and said she didn't want to hear that. He got loud and kept saying the man approached him and said he was my father. After several exchanges of words, he began to cry. I was holding the phone in total shock. She kept her cool and insisted she didn't know what he was talking about but didn't give a shit since they were both "pissheads" and could do nothing to help her. I was sixteen at the time. She insisted he was just mad because they had recently ordered him to pay $144 a month for child support. I took her side, talked some mess to him too, and left it at that.

When I went to pick up money from him a few weeks later, he had tears in his eyes and said he was sorry. I was short with him and told him I would not take a paternity test but he could go to my doctor's office and get samples of my blood if he wanted to. My mother definitely said she would not be wasting her time taking a test. She responded as if the whole thing was totally absurd and deserved no attention from any of us. His girlfriend came to me that day with tears in her eyes and told me I looked just like the man. Regina cursed her out and told her to leave me alone. Sheree told me his face was my face and that he lived right around the corner from them. She truly believed I needed to see him to believe what they were saying. I refused. The situation never even came up in my mother's family. It was so silly that it was overlooked by anyone who knew the deal.

After some time passed, nobody brought it up anymore. I joined the KYARNG during my junior year of high school on delayed entry and was due to leave for basic training on the day after my eighteenth birthday. I wanted to join the air force but was forced to choose the army when the recruiters refused to help me at the air force. I had reservations regarding basic training with the army. I was told it would be hard and knew it would be difficult to be away from my family. My mother threw me a big eighteenth birthday party, complete with a cake that had my ROTC picture on it.

The next morning, I reported to the federal building for processing and was sent back home due to psychological stressors the doctors felt would hinder me in the field. I was advised to seek therapy for the things from my childhood which were apparently affecting my physical wellness. I was happy to remain home. I dated my then boyfriend Mike G. for a few more months before that fizzled out. I ran into Lando one winter day and visited him at his mother's apartment. It was casual for me, but I could tell he was still where he was three years earlier. We were intimate and I left vowing not to see him again.

THANKS FOR MY CHILD
1992

I started seeing this guy named George socially with a group of mutual friends. He wasn't really my type but we had a similar sense of humor and hanging out was fun and a great way to take my mind off of family stressors. He was really into me but I had a hard time seeing him as more than "something to do" during the hard times. We eventually became intimate and well, we've all seen that movie before…

I found out I was pregnant in May 1993 and was blown away. It could potentially be a struggle for me to keep the baby. I was trying to get prepared to go to college, he was not on my list of people to conceive with, and I still had my hands full looking after my younger sister throughout my mother's illness.

After much debate, I decided to keep my baby. I felt I was a little selfish and she would be exactly what I needed to bring some consistency to my life. My little sister was ecstatic to have her first niece and my mother wasn't too mad when she found out. I wasn't dealing with George too much anymore when I found out I was pregnant, but news of the baby gave him false hope.

George and I did not get along for most of the pregnancy. I moved onto the college campus and tried to start my college career. When I was about five months along, the doctor changed my due date. At that point, it looked like I may have been pregnant by my childhood sweetheart Lee. We never dated seriously as adults but would meet up every now and then for "old times sake." I saw him out one night and his friend asked how far along I was and jokingly asked if I was pregnant by Lee. We laughed it off, but I asked him to meet me outside and subsequently, I let him know the due date changed, and he could possibly be the baby's father. Rightfully it caught him off guard, but he was totally cool. We agreed that if the baby looked like him or anything definitive pointed to him as the father, we'd handle it. I was honest with George as well and excited thinking that would free me of him. He insisted the baby was his and continued to harass me. I caught him in the bed with a female during the pregnancy and decided then that he would not be a factor where I was concerned.

He left town during the last part of the pregnancy and was unresponsive when called about the birth.

I gave birth to Janea during the winter of 1993. I stayed at my mother's apartment to have help shortly after the birth but there was so much going on at the time. Mama constantly hounded me about why the baby's father was a no-show. I frankly didn't care and was fine moving on without him. He made no attempts to see Janea nor help with anything for her. My mother had recovered from her cancers by that time but was taking narcotics heavily for the pain. Regina was hanging out at my mother's house and envious of the care my mother gave me and the baby. They would have words and she would put her out. After my daughter was born, Regina gave birth to a son six months later.

Mama was feeding the baby large bowls of cereal and spoons of sugar for hiccups. I was told how she over fed me as an infant (which led to several stomach issues) and did not want that for my baby. I decided to go home to the apartment I moved into shortly before I had Janea. It was a cozy little spot just big enough for the two of us. We went home and began our life together.

My mother and stepfather ended up on drugs pretty bad during my daughter's first couple of years of life. It was hectic because I had a younger sister, Ann, who I worried about. I did not want her to see what my older sister and I saw as kids. I ended up bringing her to live with us.

George didn't lay eyes on Janea for months. He made jokes and said she looked like the mailman. Lee came over to meet her and said he could see she looked like George. I agreed. We spent time together off and on during her first three years and people even asked me if she was his. She was really cute like Lee, but she looked like her daddy. We always maintained that if anything changed, we would get a paternity test. However, I saw no need. Her daddy didn't want to help with her and definitely would not when I let him know he had no chance with me. He would come around here or there and I'd let him stay overnight but noticed he took no interest in Janea. He would make her cry and say mean things about her until I clocked out and made him leave. His lack of emotional connection to her was obvious and he didn't seem intent to develop one if it didn't include him having me.

Janea got sick and the prescription was over one hundred dollars. When I called him for help, he told me he wasn't giving it to me and that he had another child who needed things. I cried and when his grandmother called to check on us, she told me she could give me half of the money for the medicine. I did not want to take any money from her but Janea was suffering and really needed the medication. I told her I would pay her back as soon as I got my money from school. She was always willing to help whenever she could and loved visiting with me and Janea. George wasn't happy about our relationship and told me to stay away from her. She said I reminded her of her granddaughters and she loved me like one. She was crazy about Janea and I appreciated that.

In March 1994, his aunt Wanda called and asked to meet Janea. During the visit, she brought Janea her first Easter outfit and several other items. She told me we were family and she'd help us however she could. We had her first Easter dinner at his cousin's house. That night, he visited asking to see her. Over the next few months, we were intimate and I found myself pregnant again. I was devastated and told him I wanted an abortion. Janea was only seven months old and there was no way I could handle two babies. He told me he would help pay for it and began to hustle up the money. He came up short and I had to use my car note to cover it. He took me to the appointment and came back to get me when it was done. He told me he would have the money by the time he returned but of course, he did not. Ultimately, I lost my car because he didn't keep his word. I told him to stay away from me moving forward and I guess it registered loud and clear. I never got the money.

Several months later, in October of that same year, I met Speedy. He taught me how to make money, how to stack it, and the importance of limiting who I let into my inner circle. His help and guidance allowed me to move into a bigger apartment, one farther from the city and out of the crime-infested neighborhood we'd been living in. George tried to pop back in the picture once he saw I was officially dating someone, but I shut it down—quickly. Speedy encouraged me to let George visit Janea but I only entertained him once because I saw that he was just being nosey and only interested in what I had going on.

When I moved, I let Speedy go because his life was moving faster than I wanted mine to go at that point. He bought me a car for my graduation from cosmetology school, furniture for my new place, and set us up to be okay. I started classes at the community college and even traded the car he bought me for a new one. Everything was falling into place.

However, I didn't know the storm was on its way…

STORM IS PASSING OVER
1996

In 1996, my grandfather died suddenly after attending a wake for his sister. It was horrible. Nobody saw it coming.

My mother spiraled and ended up back on drugs. I loaned her my car and she never returned with it. When I called to see where she was, she responded that she didn't have the car. I found out she had pawned it for drugs. I was livid! I needed my car to take my daughter to daycare and go to school. She was nonchalant and simply said she didn't know where it was. I had a friend pick me up and drive me around until I found it.

My mother dried out some months later and ended up at my house. My younger sister, Little Ann, was in middle school and also living with us. She'd stayed with Regina briefly until Regina got mad over money mama wouldn't give her and Little Ann spilling polish on her couch. She cursed her out and sat her things on the front porch, leaving her in tears. Regina's good friend called and told me Little Ann was out on the porch crying because Regina was being nasty to her so I should come get her. When I got there, Regina was hostile and trying to fight me but I simply put Little Ann and her things into the car and drove off. After a few weeks, my aunt took her because she didn't want me to be burdened with my daughter and sister.

* * *

Before the flood of March 1997, Little Ann and my mother came to stay the weekend at my place. After the flood, we lost our apartment and I lost my new car. My mother and sister went to stay with my grandmother, but she was unable to take us all. My daughter and I went from place to place nightly. For some strange reason, no one seemed to keep us for more than one night. I'd leave early in the morning for work, and when I got off and called to come back, no one answered. This went on for several nights. Then, one night I drove around until after 11 PM and realized we were homeless. The car was moist from the rain and we were getting sick from the mold and humidity. Tony, a very special friend of mine, called that night and told me to come to his place. He bought us warm clothes, cooked dinner for us, and let us stay with him that night. He offered for us to return but we did not.

DOUBLE OR NOTHING
1997

My aunt was deployed during the flood and when she heard about me and my baby going from place to place, she gave me the code to her garage and told me to stay at her place. I was happy to finally have one stable location to call home.

We didn't hear much from George while we were at our new apartment but after the flood, I started seeing him out and about. When I asked for money to help us get a place, he suggested we go stay with him and his family in Radcliff, Kentucky. That was the most absurd thing I'd ever heard because I didn't know his mother and didn't want to go that far away to live.

In January 1998, after weeks of begging from him, I decided to go ahead and try staying with him at his mother's house. It was rough from the start. He appeared happy to have us there but still assumed no parental responsibility. His mother helped out a great deal with Janea and seemed to bond with her right away.

For a brief period, I moved into an apartment in the area. George came by and stayed here and there, but nothing consistent. One day while my daughter and her godmother Nicole were napping, I left to take out the trash. The apartments were seedy and had issues but we were tired of going from house to house, so I took it. Every now and then, the door would shut tight and get stuck. On my way to take out the trash, I went to shut it but remembered it was messed up and didn't want to get locked out while Janea and Nicole were sleeping. I opened it back up and it shut again. I tried to turn and walk away but noticed I was stuck. I looked down to find bright red blood dripping from the door. Unbeknownst to me, the door had slammed on my hand. After several seconds of fighting to get it open, I ran to the sink.

As the cold water ran down my hand, I noticed my fingertip was hanging off. I guess I was in shock because I didn't feel a thing! The blood made me nauseous and dizzy. I called a few family members and set off to the emergency room. My aunts, uncles, grandmother, and friend were all there to meet me. The staff wrapped my hand in a wash rag and told me to wait. My grandmother was fuming at the fact that

I had to sit in pain. I ended up waiting for *four hours* before being seen. They told me I needed a penicillin shot and I went off. My grandmother came back with me and laughed when the nurse told me I'd have to get the shot in my rear. My grandmother held my hand through it, they sewed my fingertip back on, and back home I went.

George started staying more to help around the house while my finger healed. I contacted a lawyer to sue the apartment for negligence which resulted in the people in the apartment's office harassing me. George reintroduced the idea of us moving to Radcliff with him again. He persisted and I gave in. Shortly before moving, we were intimate and I found out a month later I was pregnant with twins.

The pregnancy was unexpected and very stressful. We were not getting along, I was unhappy there, and I yearned to be back home with my family. I wasn't working at the time and had no money to cover the expense of terminating the pregnancy. He would lead me to believe that he would give me the money but then refuse to do so whenever I didn't do what he wanted me to do. During the time we lived together, he was cruel to our daughter and became verbally and physically abusive towards me during the pregnancy. I had to leave him and that environment. I moved out when I was six months pregnant and ended up prematurely giving birth to twin boys shortly after.

For two months, the twins fought for their lives before being released from the hospital. George was in jail when they were born and even when he got out, refused to visit them during that entire time. His mother took care of Janea whenever I went to the hospital. We stayed with her for almost one year but George became abusive again, to both me and my daughter, so one day in June 1999, I packed up my children and returned home.

Speedy had gone to prison during the time of the flood. He got out after I had the twins and had been trying to contact me. When he heard about the situation I was in, he offered to help me move back home. I initially stayed at my sister's house for a weekend. She was dating a good friend of Speedy's, so it seemed to be okay. However, she was secretly vindictive about my relationship with Speedy and the luxuries it afforded me on a platonic level. I learned from my mother that she was saying nasty things about me, so we left her house. My mother urged us to come stay at her place because my sister's house was crowded. We changed locations and mom was happy to have us there.

But, not for long…

THREE'S COMPANY
1999

One weekend, we went out shopping for a family reunion and mama seemed to be in a bad mood because we had been out. She started fussing about the utilities being too high with us there and needing money for her bills. I offered money when I moved back, and she said no. She wanted to "help" us. Unfortunately, when it looked like I was doing too well, "help" had a whole price tag attached to it.

After that instance, she remained combative. One night, I wanted to go out and have some fun after the stress of the move and she agreed to watch the kids. George showed up demanding to speak to me and she let him in against my wishes. I continued to get dressed and acted as if he wasn't there at all. When I got ready to go, he was sitting down holding one of the babies. I asked her why she was letting him stay and she said it was okay for him to sit with his kids.

Her crib, okay…

I left and he proceeded to blow up my phone for hours asking when I was coming back. I assured him not at all as long as he was there. When my friend drove me home later that night, his car was still parked outside. Instead of dropping me off, I told her to keep going. I called my mother to let her know I wasn't coming back until he left but she didn't answer. I went on to my friend's house and fell asleep.

Early the next morning, my mother was livid and called cursing me out about leaving the kids with her. I tried to explain that I wasn't coming back with him there. She knew he had been abusive to me but didn't care and chewed me out because it was the day she paid her bills and she couldn't do so with the kids there. Truthfully, she could have gone because my younger sister was now fifteen years old.

I had my friend take me home and was horrified to see that he was still there. I called my mother to ask why he was still there. She told me he'd stayed with his kids. For clarity, my mother could not stand him. Right then I knew things could only get uglier. She told me to get inside and get my kids so she could leave. I told her their daddy was there so he could stay with them while she ran her errands. But then I thought about it and did not want him alone with my sister. I said goodbye to my friend and went on in the house.

He answered the back door and mushed my head as I came in. We had a little back and forth at the door and she never even came to see what was going on. She fussed some more and then got her things to leave. As soon as the door closed behind her, he started interrogating me about where I'd stayed. At first, I argued back but then decided it was best not to engage him. I wasn't sure how far he'd go and since she left us there with him, I was in a bind. I had to bite my tongue and do what I had to do to keep me and my kids safe. I asked him to just leave and he would not. He was angry and clearly wanted a battle. I called my grandmother to let her know what was going on and she told me to call the police if he insisted on staying so I did. I told George they were coming but he said he wasn't going to leave. In the end, he left before the police arrived.

I guess one of the neighbors called my mother to let her know the police was there. She went off on me! Told me I knew better than to call the police to her house and I needed to get my kids and leave. I couldn't believe she was so angry when I was clearly in danger. She'd called and had the guy who fought my sister sent back to prison so her reaction was weird and concerning. *Did she want me to be hurt?* When George was good to me, she couldn't stand him. Now all of a sudden, she tolerated his mistreatment of me. She told me to be gone before she got back so I woke my sister up to let her know we were leaving. Then, I went back to my aunt's house again.

That weekend, my dad's sister Gee called to ask why I told her ex's wife who she was and where she lived. I knew nothing about what she was accusing me of. My dad was with her and actually called me for her. I was totally ambushed and tried to explain to her that I had nothing to do with any of it. She cursed and yelled at me about my mouth and kept saying I ought to be glad they kept me. I was clearly confused as to why she kept saying that. She proceeded to tell me that I was not his daughter. I blew her off as a drunk lunatic and hung up on her. She and my mother were cool, so I mentioned it to her. She blew it off too and said they were crazy and talking shit. I was twenty-three at the time. I never connected it to the phone call I overheard when I was sixteen. It did piss me off though, so I detached myself from my dad's family. I was upset she'd accused me of something I knew nothing about.

After about a month, one of my dad's exes, Sheere, reached out to me because my grandmother was upset that she hadn't heard from me. I told her what happened and said I wasn't interested in speaking to them. Sheree was the woman he'd been with at the time of the original phone call, but she didn't mention it again. Over the years when she dated my dad, we bonded and I even stayed with them when I was fourteen and during one of those weekends Janea and I fled George's place. She appealed to my heart and convinced me that I needed to speak with my grandmother. My dad was with someone else at the time but Sheere started coming back around to get to know the kids. I would later learn why she felt the need to do so…

My grandmother told me not to entertain anything Gee said and reiterated how much she loved me and knew I hadn't done what I was accused of. Time went on and so did I. We stayed with my aunt for a few months until I was able to find an apartment of my own in the winter of 1999. My mother had secured herself an apartment, got my sister back, and entered a relationship with a really sweet guy named Rich. Rich was a family man and loved children. I had always had great rapport with my mother's partners, and he was no different. He loved my kids and she would allow them to come over on a regular basis.

BLACK BUTTERFLY
2001

I was going to the club regularly while in school and dating here and there. Through a brief romance with a guy named Smith in 2001, I became pregnant. I was on birth control at the time. He didn't want to have a child, and I wasn't crazy about the idea either. My dad was staying with me due to his drug and alcohol issues, so I was on overload. George was in a better state with the boys. He would pick them up, take them to school, and keep them on weekends. The downside to that was, he would have nothing to do with our daughter. He would not allow her to go with him and drove off most times with her standing at the car crying.

Smith and I decided to terminate the pregnancy and whatever we called our situation at the time. He paid half for the procedure, so I wasn't financially burdened. I did not want to have another abortion, so I was hit hard afterwards. I prayed and relied on my support system to get myself back together.

I ended up connecting with a younger guy at a party whom I had known for many years named Pepe. He had a crush on me and now was confident in his approach. We talked on the phone a great deal and he would stop by to visit here and there.

STING LIKE A BEE
2001-2002

In September of that year, I lost my grandmother. She was a critical part of my life and the blow was tremendous.

Regina and I lived in the same apartment complex and she started having issues with me and my kids. She told my mother it wasn't "fair" that their daddy gave me money. Janea had a necklace from her daddy but Regina's son broke it while Janea was at her house visiting. I didn't give it any attention because they were playing, and I didn't buy it. My sister wanted to argue about it and make it a big deal, but I refused to. When I ignored her, she went off. She started calling my house repeatedly leaving violent messages and challenging me to a fight. My mother was stranded from a trip to the Bahamas during the 9/11 crisis so I had to call my aunt to intervene. She tried to talk to her, asking her not to keep harassing me. No deal. She continued to call and even told me she would "go to jail and catch a case for me." I was not shocked because she had done many heinous things to me as a child and even held a gun to my head at thirteen telling me she would kill me. She had an ongoing jealousy that reared its ugly head more often than not. She could be protective of me at times, but when this side of her came out, it was unnerving.

By now I was completely fed up with it. She had no true reason to keep acting that way. I did nothing but help her and her kids. My mother often fueled the fire by talking about me to her and sending her to me to deal with issues that her mother should have handled. So, when my grandmother passed, we were not speaking. I made a conscious decision to let it all go as we grieved her loss.

My mother came back and tried to talk to her about how she was behaving. It didn't last long, though. The day my grandmother died, they hung out and due to some kind of vendetta against me, took my luggage to my grandmother's back yard instead of bringing it to me at my house. She was in the house alone and no one knew.

Pepe was a really good guy and very kind to me and my kids. My sister and mother didn't take too well to that. There were several other members of both his and my family who seemed to have an issue with our relationship. I began to stay to myself and dealt only with my close aunts and sister-friends.

I opted not to attend my grandmother's funeral. I couldn't stand the thought of watching so many people mourn her who did not take time out to be with her during her illness and last days. We were very close and I visited with her several times a day.

After the dust settled, my aunts began the tedious task of cleaning out her house. They would get together and work in the house but there were three siblings who caused mayhem throughout the process.

One day, they went to the store to get items for the house. Three of my aunts went into the store while my mother and her sister stayed in the car. I'm not sure how it happened but my aunt's phone called me. When I answered, no one responded to me saying hello. After repeated requests, I stopped because I could hear talking. It was my mother and her older sister talking and they were talking about me. They discussed me having "all those kids" and how I thought I was "all that." They said my other aunts kissed my ass and catered to me and my kids. My aunt also spoke about the daughter she had that she didn't like.

I could not believe my ears. They were so evil

when speaking and sounded like they hated my guts. I had done nothing to them, so it really hit hard. I hung up the phone and waited to call back when I could reach my Mainty. They were appalled and really not understanding what I was trying to tell them. None of us knew why or how that phone called me. My mother and aunt both denied saying what I know I heard. Mama showed up at my door beating and banging demanding I let her in. I refused and asked her to leave my home. She was very confrontational and after witnessing her and Regina fight for more than ten years, I knew I would not let her take me there. Regina ended up coercing her to leave.

I was pregnant at the time and found out about three weeks after my grandmother died. The news got worse…I found out I was pregnant with twins again! That really sent me down a dark path. I couldn't imagine having five kids at the same time. My aunt, who is a twin, was overjoyed and sure that her mama had sent me those babies. I was not where she was—emotionally, mentally, or physically. The medical staff was blown away that I was pregnant for the second time with twins and told me God blesses a truly special person to carry twins twice. My shock and grief would not let me see the bright side of the situation.

Pepe was having problems with the mothers of his kids and his parents and I was deeply depressed about my grandmother. My mother continued to wreak havoc but I refused to deal with her. I had met several new people in my classes at school. Tina was a beautician who moved here from another state. Her spirit and presence were so calming. Anytime I said something negative, she'd counter with something positive. There was also a nun named Jackie in our class. We hit it off and she would offer to pray for me. I couldn't believe I was actually friends with a nun! I don't know where I would've been without them though. Just as I was beginning to absorb the idea of my growing family, I started having complications with the pregnancy. I had to be hospitalized in January of 2002 and given a cerclage due to pre-term labor. I was in the hospital for five days and put on bedrest when I got home. I had to complete my schoolwork from the bed.

I tried to take it easy and Pepe moved in to help with the kids. I thought I was doing okay but on February 20, 2002 I started to feel some leaking. I called the doctor's office and was told it was probably just urine and I shouldn't worry. She advised me to rest until my next appointment. I tried for two days and on February 22, 2002 I had cramping throughout the day. This time I went straight to the ER and did not call the doctor until I was admitted. A specialist came in and told me an infection was setting up in my wound and would make it impossible to carry the babies to term. My doctor came in certain I had not followed her instructions for bedrest but was shocked to find the stitch still in place upon examination.

I had to decide whether or not to deliver the babies that night or try to wait two weeks in the hospital. I was told there was no possibility for the babies to survive the two weeks and waiting could kill me. I decided to go ahead and move forward in order to deliver and get back home to my kids. The doctor came in to cut the stitch and from there, they would let nature take its course. I'd had a dream about the gender of the babies but had no knowledge prior to that night of what they were. After getting an ultrasound, I was told one was a girl. My heart fluttered. Janea wanted a sister or two so I knew the news would really make her happy.

The next morning, I delivered two babies at 9:44 AM with Pepe holding my hand. The first baby came out kicking and moving around a lot but I couldn't hear her cries. They rushed her off to the NICU and four minutes later, another girl came out. She wasn't as active as the first and they immediately started working on her in the room. I was exhausted from the delivery, so Pepe and Regina stood close to the baby as they worked. They took her to the NICU, and I tried to get some rest.

When I was able to go see them, they were as tiny as my other twins had been but even more fragile. We couldn't hold them, but it was wonderful to be able to watch them through the incubators. I named them Jameah and Jamae. Jameah was holding her own but Jamae was not. She was struggling to breathe, and they did not expect her to survive for long. I was strong and continued to pray and rely on God to see me through. I was told they wouldn't even be born alive, so this was a blessing in itself. They were fighters out of the gate and against the odds.

I called my pastor in to pray with us and we went to the NICU together. Pepe had gone home to check on the kids and come back in a lucid state. This was new to him and he really struggled with the whole process of letting our baby go. I went back to my room after the prayer and dozed off. Somewhere in the early morning of February 24, 2002, Jamae Sheree Collier passed away. I was sad but rejoiced because it was my grandmother's birthday. What a precious gift for her to receive!

It truly was bittersweet. I didn't have much time to sit in it though because there was still a baby to see to and my family at home. The doctor came in and said we knew it would happen, which was terribly inconsiderate, insensitive and rude. I asked her to let me go home a day early. I needed to be with my kids and as usual, no one who said they would look after them, did so. They passed them around from place to place with no regard for what we were going through. I guess Regina let my mother know the babies were born and one had passed away because she randomly showed up at the hospital. I let her know I was okay, but my spirit really didn't want her there. She went to the morgue and got the dead baby. I told her I did not want to see the baby again and she brought her back to my room anyway. She had my daughter with her, and I thought that was sick. She held the baby in blankets as if she was alive and even had my sister to take pictures of her holding the baby. She had my daughter pose next to them. She tried to bring the baby to the bed, and I had to tell her twice to move away. My mind could not adjust to why she would even try to do that. I know now that the trauma from that day contributed to Janea unraveling as time went on. I was able to go home later that day and start the grieving process, healing process, mothering, and consoling process for many people.

At home, I began the journey into the reality ahead. I felt bad at how much I considered getting rid of the babies when I found out I was having twins. I felt bad that I doubted how strong I really was, and that God would provide a way out of no way. I was so sad without my grandmother and the state of our family since she passed away.

Over the next few days, we planned a funeral for Jamae. Many family and friends stopped by to check on me and the kids. I still visited Jameah daily while preparing to say goodbye to her twin. Pepe had an infant daughter at the time and was embroiled in a custody battle with her mother. I spent time with her when she visited and found joy in doing so. He seemed to be sinking into an abyss of grief and all of these new situations that he'd never been in before. He drank and smoke to numb the pain and I kept busy. I started looking for premature baby clothes for when Jameah got better and came home. After Jamae's service, Jameah started to deteriorate. She had contracted an infection that was making an already difficult situation worse. Her little body just couldn't take much more. I started preparing myself for what was to come while shuddering at the thought that I had gone through all of that to end up with no babies at all. Funny how life can serve you up on a platter. The term "watch what you wish for" was kicking my ass. I realized that when I had my first abortion in 1994, I got a set of twins in 2001. Now here we were March 2002, and my second set was left with one very fragile baby.

After ten days of fighting as much as her little body could, Jameah Ron'ja Collier, exited this life. The doctors called the night before and said they could intubate. That made me sick to my stomach because her body was so tiny, and I couldn't imagine someone opening up that little body and trying to stick tubes in it. I had my pastor pray with us again and told the doctor by phone to remove the ventilator. I knew she would pass sometime during the night, but the doctor told me they would let me know exactly when. Bless her soul…she fought on for hours once the ventilator was removed and passed early the next morning.

Our family was devastated. We all looked forward to the joy of twin girls to lift our spirits, but it seemed that the darkness was going to be around a while longer. The funeral home was so sweet. When I called to make the arrangements for Jameah, they told me that they held a spot next to her sister for her. That made an unbearable situation a little better. We had a service for Jameah shortly after and tried to make peace with God's plan. I was not bitter at all and thanked God for the opportunity to walk through yet another obstacle in my life and come out standing.

Jackie and Tina were truly Godsends. The nuns from her order put together a huge box of baby things and we had already started buying baby clothes. I remember going into the closet one day to see what I needed to take back to the store and I just collapsed on the floor with sadness. Things were moving so fast that I wasn't truly able to grieve. Not my grandmother, my babies, Sheree, who passed away from Cancer in June 2001, nor my two cousins who committed suicide three months apart in 2000. I was sexually violated by a distant family member after the death of my second cousin. This was a great deal to digest but I stayed in protection mode of those around me and often neglected to protect myself. There was beginning to be a pattern of pregnancy after grief.

After the deaths of the girls, I was pretty much done with Pepe. He was spiraling from all of the different things he had going on outside of our relationship. His parents were utterly dysfunctional and used him as a crutch when they failed to handle business in their home. His kids had nasty vindictive mothers who were jealous and used their kids as pawns to get even. Some of his boys were jealous of him and leading him down a path that would only hurt him. Pepe also had some paternity issues in his life that he attempted to deal with but could not fully due to backlash from his parents. There was not much room for me to deal with the foolishness from both of our lives. I told myself that since the babies were gone, he needed to go too. That idea didn't sit well with him at all and he cried to stay. He promised he'd do better and try to bring some order to the continuing chaos in his life.

I blocked the people out of my life who continued to bother me and my well-being. My family kept saying we needed to have another baby because we were all so sad. I didn't think so because I was still reeling from the past few months. I cried so much about my grandmother being gone. We were extremely close, and she was part of my daily routine for so many years. She wasn't in the best of health and was tired of feeling like a burden to her children so I respected her right to move on where life wouldn't be so hard but it sure did hurt.

SUNSHINE AFTER THE RAIN
2002

I decided I would go on and get back on birth control when I went back to see my doctor in June. Pepe and I were doing a little better and we had a great Memorial Day celebration with our neighbors and friends. His daughter turned one that week but there was still plenty of hell from her mother.

I tried to help him maneuver around the BS and still remain a father to his child, but they were really getting on my nerves with the childish antics back and forth. When I went to the doctor in June for my birth control, I found out I was pregnant again. I had mixed feelings and wasn't sure the time was right. I had pretty much decided that Pepe was done and was ready to move on. The family was happy to hear about the pregnancy as were my older kids. The twins were turning four that month and my oldest was eight. We sure could use some joy right about now but I was terrified of being pregnant with twins and it ending in a loss. My doctors assured me it was only one baby and I would be okay.

Four months into the pregnancy, we decided to move into our first house. Pepe was hanging out with his friends and ended up getting arrested the night before. He had been on home incarceration during the summer months and had just gotten off in the fall. I warned him about hanging out with people who put him at risk. He could be really gullible and didn't make good decisions when around his friends. It worried me that they were okay going against what I was trying to tell him for his own good and seemed to enjoy watching him fall.

He was able to get out the next day and we started moving. He was in a pitiful mood all day because he knew I was upset. As we waited for the furniture delivery, my dad pulled me to the side. He told me to take it easy on Pepe and said he felt really bad about what he'd done.

Well duh! He should! That actually made me more upset. Pepe was a twenty-three-year-old version of him! I'd already seen the movie and did not think too kindly of repeats. But it definitely occurred to me that I had started dating my father. Pepe was a blend of my dad and my stepfather.

I was still taking classes at U of L as we moved and got settled into our new place. Now that I was pregnant again and we were looking to move up in the world, things got worse for Pepe with his family and his baby mamas. He was catching hell every which way he turned. He hung out late at night and usually came home under the influence of something. That quickly got tiring and I had to clock out on him. I urged him to go back to his mother's place, but she wanted to keep his father there instead of him. He seemed to really be hurting with that situation and I found it hard to make him leave. He would try to get it together when I started fussing but it didn't last.

Both of his baby mamas created more conflict and lost their minds at the very thought of me having a child by him. The closer I got to my delivery, the worse they behaved! Meanwhile, George was cooking up his own pot of poison for the impending delivery. After almost two years of him refusing to take Janea on visits, I stopped letting him take the boys. I saw no reason for her to continue to be subjected to that pain. In response, he filed charges against me for keeping the boys and took me to court. The day before I had the new baby, I was in court in front of a judge being berated and threatened with jail time for contempt of court. The judge would not even consider what I was saying about him refusing to take Janea when he picked up the boys. They set a visitation schedule of which he very lightly abided by.

Our son Khy was born in February of 2003. He was such a beautiful blend of Jameah and Jamae. Just what we needed. He was the most peaceful baby. We took care of him together, took turns feeding him, and changing diapers. Pepe was a wonderful partner. He also took the other three kids to school, fed them, and provided for them financially.

I was back in school to obtain my bachelor's degree. I worked as a work study student and met my friend, Vicki. She was younger than me but very mature. I took Khy in to work with me one day and she fell in love with him. She started spending a great deal of time with our family. Her family lived in a neighboring city, so we were close by. Her mother and sister came in town to visit and fell in love with Khy as well. They began taking him to their home and keeping him regularly. He loved having that time to himself to be spoiled. We spoiled him terribly at home as well, given he was the first child born after the death of the girls.

PROMISE TO LOVE
2006

The semester before my graduation, Pepe proposed. I was caught off guard by it and really not too excited about getting married. It was starting to be a task to be with him and keeping him away from himself. I agreed to marry him and talked to him about what he needed to do to be in alignment with the plans I had for our family. He got a really good job and started to get into formation with the plan. Our intimate life picked up because I could see him more as a man and not a boy I needed to continuously lead around and make decisions for.

As luck would have it, I found out I was pregnant two months before the wedding and my graduation. I was getting really sick and even vomited during classes. It was clear, this one was going to be rough. I spoke to Pepe about it and told him it wouldn't be a good time to have another baby. He seemingly agreed and we terminated the pregnancy. I knew abortions should not be treated as a form of birth control and pledged to God it would be the last one. I was so thankful when Khy was born healthy and the other kids were healthy, so this was troubling. I prayed and asked for forgiveness with the choice I made. Pepe had never experienced an abortion with anyone and started drinking more. His behavior put me in a mood and we argued. He stayed out all night and I put him out when he returned the next day. He swore that he was at his mother's house and meant no harm. I didn't care. That gave me just what I was looking for—a way to get him away for good. Except it wasn't. He managed, with the help of several of my family and friends, to convince me to let him come back home.

He had lost his grandfather earlier that year and we truly had been through a great deal. The wedding was scheduled for May 2006 as was my graduation from college. We went ahead with both. My mother and her latest husband, Felder, came to the graduation and bought me a washer and dryer as a gift. It was a combination gift for the graduation and the wedding. Felder was a cash cow and denied my mother nothing financially. She and my two sisters reaped all the benefits while I may have received a birthday gift here and there.

Regina was pregnant and on the outs, looking for a reason to be angry. Mama reported her to Child Protective Services (CPS), for reasons unknown to me this day, and ended up with her two youngest kids. I was asked to be listed as an emergency contact if anything happened to mama and blamed for the call.

Shortly before the wedding, my mother fell in her condo and broke her jaw. I brought her to my house after the surgery to care for her. It was hard having her in my home. She constantly made comments about what we had like she wasn't happy with my independence. She talked about her unhappiness with her husband and insinuated there may be some abuse taking place. Against my better judgment, she went back home before the doctor recommended. She said she was going to stay with her husband.

She opted not to attend the wedding which we had in Gatlinburg, Tennessee. My dad told us he would come but disappeared on the day of without any notice. He had recently celebrated sobriety for an extended period of time and seemed to look forward to going with us. For whatever reason, he was not there. My twin boys walked me down the aisle, Janea was a bridesmaid along with my younger sister and Victoria, and Khy was the ring-bearer. Pepe's parents and grandmother came down to support him and we had a really good time with several of my aunts and cousins coming to celebrate our union.

About two months after the wedding, Regina went into the hospital with complications from her pregnancy. While hospitalized, her first child's father was brutally murdered. It hit us all very hard because he was like a brother to me. We grew up together and shared a love for my nephew. Plus, I'd introduced them. I was by my nephew's side while Regina gave birth to the new baby and his father was laid to rest.

By the time the baby was born, things settled down some. I visited with my new niece and helped out like always regardless of how I was treated. Mama and her husband did a great deal financially for my two sisters throughout their marriage. I asked for a loan to buy schoolbooks, about $48 and told my mother I would pay it back when I got my school loan. She did so begrudgingly and said I had to make sure and pay her back. It was a good week before I started hearing through the grapevine that I owed her money and was taking too long to pay it back. I could not believe my ears! The one time I asked for help and barely got it, I had to hear about it from everyone else! I ended up having Pepe pay her back right then to kill that noise.

Sometime later, I had a wreck in a rental car and was afraid I would be dropped if I reported it to my insurance company, so I called mama crying asking for $700 to have the car fixed before I turned it in. She adamantly told me no and that her husband did not have any money. I had access to his accounts and knew there were thousands of dollars in it. She told me she had recently paid her brother to paint her condo and would not be asking him for any more money. She told me she was sorry I was crying but could not help me. I was devastated. Again, here I was, the child who achieved and never needed assistance with bills, kids, etc. and was still being treated like an unwanted nuisance. I figured it out on my own like I always did and moved on.

LIFE IMITATES ART
2006

After the wedding, I was in school and spending a great deal of time watching soap operas. General Hospital was my drug of choice and I remember being so enthralled in the storyline where Elizabeth Webber had a baby by Jason Morgan but she was married to Lucky Spencer, so she kept it a secret. Jason was around the baby all the time and forming a bond with it. Elizabeth was torn and miserable in her marriage trying to keep the secret.

Pepe would watch with me and it was hilarious to see a man so caught up in the story. Meanwhile, he was really struggling with the unfinished paternity issues he faced. I learned about an online DNA test you could order for free and send back to be analyzed. I loved trying new things, so I had the bright idea to order one just to see how they work and if they really worked. I spoke to Pepe about it and he said he would try the test first. He got it and never did. I'm more action-oriented so I decided to order one myself to take with my father.

In hindsight, I realized that something was off because I told my father I was doing a project for school and needed him to take the test with me. He didn't resist right out but seemed a little hesitant about taking it. When I finally got him to come over, he appeared really tense. My stepmother encouraged him to go ahead and we swabbed our cheeks. I sent the packet off the next day and told him I would let him know when I got the results. I selected the option to receive the results by email. For several weeks, I would come home every day checking my email to see if anything came. Nothing. After about three weeks, I stopped looking and carried on with my life.

On March 29, 2007, I was called in to sub at an elementary school. It was Regina's birthday. The day was hard, and I was quite tired when I got home. I sat down at my computer after taking my shoes off and started checking the emails. I noticed "Genetic Tree" or something like that in the sender line as soon as I opened the page. I paused for a second to place what exactly the email was about. By that time, the paternity test had totally slipped my mind. When I clicked to open the email, I suddenly had butterflies in my stomach and a little cramping. I couldn't figure out why my body was sending signals of anxiety, but I read through the results. I knew a little about reading them because I made Pepe take one for our baby. I knew how gullible he could be and decided that if we ever split up and a woman tried to convince him that Khy wasn't his, we'd be covered.

I read down the individual columns and look at the numbers. I knew there should be a pattern where the child either has similar numbers to the mother, father, or both parents. Being that my mother didn't participate, I was only left with me and my daddy to compare. I noticed that none of our numbers were the same. There seemed to be no compatibility whatsoever. I kept hope as I scanned down to the last number. In the closing paragraph it read: "There is 0% probability that the above listed is the father."

I read that line over and over again. The percentage never changed. I knew it was bad because the test I took with Pepe said 99.7% probability. My heart froze at that moment. I could not believe my eyes. I had so many things going through my head. Who should I call? What would I say? Why didn't I know this already? And then I broke down crying. I thought about my father and his sobriety and decided I would not be able to tell him the news. I called my aunt Jean who is his sister and shared the information with her. I swore her to secrecy and hoped it would stay there. Meanwhile, I called my mother's sisters and my little sister to share the news with them. Everyone was in shock and disbelief. None of us saw it coming.

Of course, my mother and I were not speaking at the time due to something involving my younger sister that my mother was jealous of. I called a good friend of hers and asked if she knew who my real father may be. She told me she was sorry to hear the news and didn't know. I asked her to let my mother know what I found out. When she failed to respond, I had my younger sister call our mother and tell her the news and see if she would tell her the name of my biological father. To my surprise, she told my sister I would "just have to get over it" and she was having nothing to do with it.

I was crushed. Here I was stuck with this life-changing information with no way of finding any closure. I cried day in and day out for my father and what the news would do to him. Now I was able to go back and see why his family treated me differently growing up. They teased me and called me names. Always said I looked like a turtle and even called my kids baby turtles when they were born. They often said he treated me like a princess, and I did not deserve it. I would see them at parks and show up with my kids to be met with, "What are you doing here? How did you find us?" making me feel like an outsider. They were always really nice and receptive to Regina though. I think it was easier to accept her because they knew she wasn't his, but I was like the fraud baby being passed off as his. My aunt Jean even told me she knew all along he wasn't my father. That was a tough blow. Jean ended up telling my grandmother and she called upset. I spoke with her and confirmed what she had heard. She just kept saying she didn't believe it. She said the tests aren't always correct and maybe we could take another one. I assured her it was accurate but could not continue to live in the myth. I had work to do.

Using the information I had from the phone call when I was sixteen, I had a name—Ray. I also remembered being about six years old and a man at the store hugging me and giving me three quarters. One of the quarters was red. He looked at me and told my mother I looked just like his daughter. When I was about ten, I remember seeing the same man at another store. When I got out, he hugged me and said to my mother again that I looked like his daughter. I went into the store and they stayed outside talking.

When I came back out, he was gone. I knew then that he was the man from the store four years earlier, so I asked who he was. She said he was some old guy she knew named Ray. I asked her why he kept saying I looked like his daughter. She told me he had a lot of kids and thought I favored one of them. Enough said right? We trust our mamas to tell us the truth. Mine never sugar coated anything. I can think of tons of things shared throughout my childhood that could've been kept from me.

I called my mother's youngest sister, Mainty, and asked if she knew who Ray was. She made a few calls and was able to give me his home address. I was planning a trip to Disney World with my kids, so I had limited time to handle things. My oldest aunt recalled a time when one of our church members came to her at church saying she was my sister. When she mentioned it to me, I was highly offended. I thought she was implying that Mick was her father and I wasn't hearing that at all. I was his only child. I had actually grown up in the same social circles as this girl, so I knew her most of my life. I tried to locate her but had no luck. I was told there were pretty good odds that I would find him at his place if I just stopped by.

My mind was all over the place the next week. I

was pissed off at Pepe because I felt like this was his fault. Trying to prove a point to him blew my whole life up and he still had no intention of rectifying his own mess. I got to the point where I couldn't stand to see his face. I had been dodging my daddy's calls for weeks and he was excited because he was getting close to receiving a settlement he'd been waiting on for years. I decided I would go to see Ray the day before we took our trip. I only shared my plans with a couple of people who offered to go with me but I knew this needed to be done on my own.

MIRROR IMAGE
2007

Me and Khy ventured off to meet Ray on May 24, 2007 while the other kids were in school. I knew he would not understand what was happening, but he was my little wingman and went everywhere with me. I was told that Ray rode a bike everywhere he went so if I saw a bike, he was home. As we pulled up, not only did I see a bike, I saw two men sitting on the porch. As I approached them, one of the men was reading a newspaper. When I walked up, he never took the paper down from his face. The other guy was pretty hard looking and I remember praying to God I was at the wrong house and if not, this was not the man who I belonged to. The man greeted me and I said hello. I asked if he knew Ray. He asked me who wanted to know, and I told him I was looking for him. He asked who I was and when I said my name, the newspaper fell, and I was staring directly into a seventy-four-year-old mirror image of my face!

He was balding and his hair was completely white. He had on glasses and I had recently started wearing glasses. It was truly a surreal moment in time. His eyes watered and he thanked the Lord right as I was standing there. I had no words. He jumped up and gave me a hug. I stood in his arms and knew right then, he was the very man I had seen twice as a child. He said he had prayed for this day and promised his mother before she passed that he would hold me in his arms. There wasn't much I could say at that point and I'm rarely speechless.

He let me go to look at me again as I stood in shock. He marveled at how pretty I was and told me he loved me. He knew so many things about my childhood and had newspaper clippings of when my twins died, my graduation, and the birth announcement for Khy. As it turns out, someone had been keeping him updated my whole life. He confirmed the run-in he had with Mick when I was sixteen. He said Mick cried and told him that he was the only father I'd ever known and that his family had helped raise me. They agreed to leave it as it was for the time being but agreed that I would be told when I was an adult. I let him know no one had told me.

He was furious with my mother. He detailed different times where he would run into us and beg her to tell me the truth. She tried to introduce him as an uncle once and he told her not to do so. If she wasn't willing to tell me he was my father, he didn't want her to tell me anything. I told him how it went down and how I found out. I also told him I really wasn't seeking him out to forge a relationship. I wanted to know who I came from and any medical information I needed to know.

We left for Florida the next day. I didn't mention it to any of my older children. I didn't know what to say. Didn't have a clue what the heck was taking place right in front of me. That night, I tossed and turned, dreaming of his face. When I woke up the next morning, I was sure I had dreamed it all. My head hurt and I was exhausted. My hope that I had dreamed the whole ordeal was shattered when the phone rang. It was an eighteen-year-old girl named Rey calling to say that she was my little sister and wanted to see me. I listened to the message in horror of what was to come.

LOVE DON'T LIVE HERE ANYMORE
2007-2008

We boarded the plane to Florida on May 25, 2007, two days before my first wedding anniversary. We left Pepe at home because I really needed to get away and clear my mind. The kids were excited to go to Disney. It was the second time for Janea and the twins and the first for Khy. I was pregnant with Khy the first time we went in 2002.

Despite the weight on my shoulders, we had a pretty good time on our trip. Mick called the day before we were to return and told me his case had been settled. I told him that was great news and we were excited for him. He said he had some money for us and he needed to talk to me when I got home. I told him I would call him when we returned.

The Saturday morning, after we returned home, I was awakened early by my friend calling telling me that her brother had committed suicide. That was sad and hard to hear. I stayed on the phone to console her but eventually, had to take Khy to his T-ball game that morning.

After we left the game, Mick called. He asked if I ever heard back from the people about the paternity test. I asked him if he had heard back. He said they sent him a letter. I asked him what it said and he wouldn't say, so I told him I received an email some months back. He asked what mine said and I asked him if he already knew the answer. He started yelling, cursing, and said something about me going to meet Ray without telling him. I thought he had the balls of a Spanish bull at that point and told him so. How dare he chastise me about exploring something so critical to my life when none of them had enough decency to tell me in the first place! He was livid and sounded like he had been drinking so whatever I said fell on deaf ears. He continued on his rant and I wasn't able to get a word in. He talked about me betraying him and having no right to let my kids meet Ray. I tried to tell him that they didn't know anything about it but could not reason with him. He hung up on me. It would be almost two years before we would speak again.

We moved through that summer as best as we could, and I lived with the weight of knowing there was another piece of the puzzle out there that I knew virtually nothing about. Several more of Ray's daughters called asking to meet me which became overwhelming. Each time I tried to make myself believe it wasn't true, another reminder came to light that it was.

Regina got sick at a family reunion in early 2007 and was rushed to the hospital. I kept her kids and made sure the two who went to school got there on a daily basis while caring for the baby with Pepe's help until she was able to come home. When the school year began in August 2007, I took a job as an ISAP instructor at the middle school I attended while working on my first master's degree. It was such an honor to work there. The best three years of my life were spent at that school. I formed many lasting bonds with students and staff as a student. Janea was a student there as well and started having issues. She acted out and even threatened to hurt herself one day when she was in the eighth grade. She had been struggling since she turned ten and I had her in counseling. During that time and increasingly, she struggled with her identity and we tried our best to give her space to grow into whomever she chose to be.

As the twins got older, they began to have problems as well, so we all went to counseling. In

2006, George was arrested and went to prison for three years. We had no knowledge of it until someone mentioned it in the barbershop in front of the twins a year after he was sentenced.

We were still seeing Ray here and there to get to know him a little better, but the older kids still did not know exactly who he was. I hadn't heard from my mother or Mick. My mother became increasingly toxic and would tell her sisters she didn't want to hear my name and was sick of them always talking about me. This was soul-wrenching. I could not understand how I was getting so much poison thrown my way when I clearly was the injured party. She likely knew my whole life as did Ray. Mick at least found out when I was sixteen and I was left in the dark for sixteen more years.

One of my cousins told me Mick took her to Ray's house and pointed him out to her. She couldn't believe how much I looked like him. When she asked Mick if he planned to tell me about Ray, he said he never would. I don't know if he ever knew the severity of that decision. He shared it with his family and that further added to the doubt they'd always had about me and the mistreatment of me and my kids. I would later learn that my kids were teased in middle and high school by "cousins" who told peers they were not really related to us, only by marriage.

* * *

I walked into the Fall of 2007 hopeful for better things and determined to get my life back on track regardless of who was on board. Shortly thereafter, my youngest sister gave birth to my niece. I prayed she would be born on my birthday, but she came nine days before both mine and her father's birthday and three days after Pepe's.

She was like a dream come true. My very own little Libra doll! I picked them up from the hospital and Pepe and I cared for her while her mother recuperated. It was an absolute pleasure to have a baby in the house again that wasn't mine! She had my name for her middle name and oddly enough, a personality early on that mirrored mine. TK was my whole heart wrapped up in a beautiful koala baby! It was reminiscent of when her mother was born and the joy I felt to be her big sister. Since I raised her mother, TK was more like a grandbaby than a niece. Whatever the case, she brought so much joy and love back to the house. Lord knows we needed it!

As happy as I was having my new niece, some old things were starting to eat away at me and needed to go. I ended up having to let a really old friend go because she was discussing the paternity situation openly at her job with strangers. I hadn't spoken to my mother yet so it was very tacky for her to be doing that. Turned out that one of her co-workers knew one of Ray's daughters and it came right back to me that she was sharing my story. I did not have any room for anymore mess than I carried on my own.

Pepe started hanging out more and took up with some unsavory characters that would likely land him in jail or worse. We had moved, I started my career, and needed to stay on course in order to make sure we kept what we had. After Christmas that year, I asked him to leave and told him I wanted to look into getting a divorce. I didn't really offer him an explanation because I didn't feel I needed to at that point. He had been given plenty of warnings over the years. He was hurt and didn't want to go. I was starting to get headaches and stress was keeping me in a bad place.

By Spring 2008, I had convinced him to go back to his mother's place. I told him I wanted him to demonstrate some independence outside of my house and we could go from there. We were technically still together but living apart. I started going to church more and he would even join us on several occasions.

My new sister, Rey, came around a lot and spent time with us. She was so smitten with me and loved having a new big sister. Apparently, Ray had several "new" daughters coming out of the woodwork. I let them know quickly it was all so new to me and I wasn't ready for all that. Too much too soon.

* * *

That summer, I graduated with my master's degree. The ceremony took place in Bowling Green which was two hours from my home. Several of my family members drove down from Louisville and even came from Georgia to see me walk across the stage. Mick nor my mother was speaking to me at the time so neither attended. Imagine my surprise when I got to the arena and received a call from Ray saying he was there with his brother. That evening, I got to meet my uncle for the first time. They gave me a card with $100 in it and stayed until the graduation ended. We took pictures together and they headed back home.

Rey and her mother came as well along with my good friend, Shanell. We stopped at a Cracker Barrel on the way home and had a big celebratory meal. Pepe didn't make it but financed the trip so we had a little extra to splurge. He was very proud of me and I was glad to have his support. Our divorce was final May 2008, two years to the day of our wedding. We were still "together" though. He seemed to be making steps in the right direction as far as his business was going.

After the graduation, I got my first teaching job at a middle school and he started coming back to the house to stay and help get the kids off to school since I had to be at work before they were awake. There was a bad windstorm in September 2008 and we were without power for five days. We went to a hotel, but Pepe was rarely there with us. Over the course of the next few months, we would get back together, but it was short-lived due to him being involved with a girl with which I shared a friend. She knew who I was and apparently wanted the life I had with Pepe.

In the midst of the mess with him and his fling, Janea started to unravel. She was now in her teen years, caught up in the mix with my mother, her father, and Regina's disdain for me. We were looking for a new home to purchase and Pepe would accompany me to some of the viewings, but I knew the purchase would be mine alone. As we maneuvered through the mistress pretending she was pregnant, him being sorry but totally blind to the fact that it was a lie and he was being manipulated, and my daughter's issues, I tried to stay sane. I went on a stress diet and lost more than thirty pounds. I was back to my high school size (which looked awesome) and trying to get my head back in the game.

By January 2009, I had played the game with Pepe longer than I needed or wanted. We had an ice storm that left us out of the house for a week. I went to the hotel and sent my kids to stay at my aunt's house. Pepe was out pretending to be at his mother's place but I saw through his lies. February of 2009, I let him go. I was tired of the mistress calling and coming to my house. He couldn't figure out where he wanted to be so I made the choice for him. I was sad and really only fighting to keep him from her. I knew I didn't want him but she was no good for him. Poor thing, he didn't even see it was more about me than him for her. She was envious and would struggle for five more years begging to have the life I had with him. No deal…

LOVE IS A HOUSE
2009

I purchased my first home on March 9, 2009. It ended up being the house one of my aunt's owned during my childhood, so I was delighted to be back. It had been fully gutted inside due to a fire so it was like new with the original foundation.

I decided I didn't want any memories from the old house, so I bought all new furniture. Pepe and I were having spats when I moved in and still reeling from the separation. He was living with the mistress by then but still begging to come back. After we got settled in that Spring, I started letting him come over to the house. He'd swear he was no longer with the mistress and back at his mother's house. We did that off and on until the fall of that year before I snapped, and someone almost got hurt. He assured me he was done with her and wanted to have his family back. He would even pick up our son and send him back saying his daddy was moving in with us.

Somewhere during that summer, George was released from prison. Much like when he went in, we knew nothing about his release. Regina said she saw him riding down the street with Janea in the car and I assured her that wasn't the case. That's how we found out he was released. When school started back that year, I had formed a bond with one of the teachers. Mrs. Shuan was going through a divorce and we took to each other as we co-taught a class. She seemed to really know how to calm me down when the mistress would have me amped up and in attack mode. Mrs. Shaun was truly a ball of fire but had the patience of Mother Theresa when dealing with morons. I hadn't learned that quite yet! Needless to say, I was nearing the point of frustration with Pepe and his inability to stay in one place or the other. In September, I again made the choice for him. I went on and let him be and decided it was time for me to move on and let them play games with each other.

I had a good friend named Tee who Pepe always talked to and called his "sister." He would confide in her and explain his desire to leave the mistress. He said he wanted to come back home, but he was intimidated by me and my refusal to connect emotionally. He was looking for that love he couldn't get at home but for me he became more like a son than my man. I had groomed him and guided him for so long that the intimacy was lost.

We went out for my birthday in October. The party started at Applebee's where we ate and started drinking. After our meal, we headed to the club. I kept seeing Tee on the phone but had no idea who she kept calling. She was doing the same thing in the club. Pepe called to wish me a happy birthday and I thanked him. After five or six tequila shots too many, I made it home and passed out.

Early the next morning, I heard my doorbell and phone ringing. It was the day before my birthday. When I got up and answered the phone, it was Pepe. He said he was at the door and had a card for me. I was still hungover from the night before but made it to the door. He came in and we talked casually. After he wished me happy birthday again, he went back to use the bathroom. The birthday gift was shared with me before he left. I wasn't too thrilled about the interaction and definitely did not feel any ties when he left. He said he was going to change his clothes and would come back later. We didn't discuss the mistress at all. He did not return and I heard nothing from him that night.

When I got up for work the next morning, I tried

to call him and he didn't answer. The mistress lived near my job so I decided to drive by on my way to work. Sure enough, his car was there. I was pissed! I wasn't mad to the point of doing anything crazy though. I was pissed at myself for falling for the birthday booty call. I went on to work, struggled through the day angry and hung over, and left to go home for part two of the celebration with my girls.

As I stopped to get gas on the way home, Tee called. She was laughing and asked if Pepe called me the night we left the party. I told her he showed up the next morning with a card. She said that was who she had been talking to that night and he was supposed to show up at the club. She encouraged him to bring the card. I started crying and told her what had happened over the past few days. She felt awful and apologized for getting involved and encouraging him to come to me when I was on my way to letting him go. I forgave her and knew without a doubt that I was ready to walk away.

OLD HABITS DIE HARD
2009-2010

October moved on and Pepe and I were co-parenting our son, Khy. He was acting out a little with the change of not seeing his daddy all the time. I would call and have Pepe pick him up for a few hours and take him to the barbershop.

One day towards the end of October, Pepe had Khy with him and I called asking him to get some cough syrup for him before bringing him back home. I hadn't been feeling good and also hadn't had a period. Ironically enough, when he came back after the divorce, we talked about having another baby but that ship had long sailed. I was learning to live without the drama contrary to what the insecure mistress tried her best to keep going as the truth.

I had some pregnancy tests in my medicine cabinet and decided to take one. When the test came back positive, I was devastated. I could not believe it!

Janea was sixteen, the twins were twelve, and Khy was seven. This was not the time for a new baby, old baby, or baby period! Yet, here I was faced with a huge moral dilemma. Remember I made a promise to God not to have any more abortions and now God was calling me to the carpet to see where I was in my walk with Him. I was so lost.

I called Pepe back and asked him to bring me some food. He said he was on the way. I went outside to get the food and when he handed me the bag, I handed him the test. In true Pepe fashion, he asked what it was.

"Uh looks like a positive pregnancy test to me," I shared with him.

"So, you saying you pregnant now?" he stammered.

I had to put a stop to this insane Q & A immediately for the safety of us all. I advised him to look at it again and fill in the blanks. He asked what I was going to do and I told him I didn't know. I left him standing there and closed the door. Sadly, there wasn't anything to consider because I knew my word was worth everything God had been doing for me all my life. I had no choice but to keep the baby.

Over the next few months, Pepe and I would go back and forth over anything and nothing at all. I think he was pissed I didn't even consider taking him back after I told him I was pregnant. After losing my twin daughters with all that stress around, I was not willing to let anyone take me there again. I prayed all day every day for the strength to walk wherever God led me and to hold my head up high. I had a wonderful village of support. Mrs. Shan, Tee, my two younger sisters, and aunts were by my side. Ray wasn't too thrilled to learn that I was having a new baby, but he didn't weigh in too heavily with a rumored nineteen plus kids of his own.

My mother had come back on the scene and almost fell out when she found out. She asked what I was going to do and I told her the same thing I'd done on my own with the previous four. By that time, Regina had moved out of town with her kids and we didn't talk much. More peace that way. However, I went to visit my cousin in the same state for Thanksgiving that year and ran into Regina while we were there. She feigned happiness while I was there and was excited to see us. She looked forward to the new baby on the way.

We tried to mend the relationship with Mick on several occasions, but he would seem okay and then blow up on me and my kids out of nowhere. Before the baby came though, we found a place of compromise. I encouraged the kids not to talk about

Granddaddy Ray around Granddaddy Mick. As they got older, I explained to them that they were both my dads, without giving too much information. It was one more person to love and receive love from as far as they were concerned so they accepted it.

They were all happy to have a new baby coming but Janea was still having issues with her identity, their dad, and following the rules of the house. I ended up sending her to a boarding school when we first moved into the house. She was there for a couple of months before being expelled. Then, I sent her to George's mother's house. That lasted for about two weeks before he began to berate her over my phone number and his mother buying her things. They ended up in a really bad argument where his mother let him put her out of the house at night so I asked my good friend's mom to go pick her up. She came back home but things were still not good so I sent her to my mom's.

Pepe tried throughout the pregnancy to get me to take him back. I had absolutely no desire to have anything more than a cordial relationship with him for the benefit of our kids. I put some items on lay-a-way for the baby and he helped pay for them. He paid for the 3-D ultrasound and I gave him a copy. I could see the baby's features in the photos!

The mistress continued to run her mouth in the streets telling people I wasn't pregnant by him. I kept right on about my business and said nothing. That summer our fourth child, Khe, was born. He was a healthy baby boy and Pepe came to the hospital that afternoon to see him. He held him, fed him, and left money for his photos before he left. I was still sure this was the way we would raise him. He was still with the mistress and she was bragging about their upcoming wedding. Better her than me!

Pepe came by the house to bring milk, diapers, and other necessities for the baby, all the while never letting the mistress know the baby was indeed his. By the time Khe was almost one, he was engaged to the mistress and she planned her wedding (still pretending the baby wasn't his) as we planned the birthday party.

In March 2011, I lost another family member to suicide. Pepe came over to offer his condolences before the wake. I decided to talk to him because he would not mention anything about the wedding and I wanted to address it and find out if he planned to include our kids. He alluded to the idea of her knowing about the baby but admitted he hadn't told her. I encouraged him to be honest with her and to be honest with himself before he married someone he'd been dishonest with throughout the relationship. He said they were in counseling and he'd bring it up.

Meanwhile, a friend told me they saw my old pal, Speedy, on Facebook. I looked him up and sent a message to say hello. I hadn't spoken to him in more than five years. We started talking and texting every day. It was good to have someone to talk to who knew me. I shared what I'd found out about my paternity and he was very comforting. He noticed the envious behavior of my mother and sister when we dated years prior so none of the attacks he'd missed out on surprised him. He encouraged me to press on and continue to thrive as I always had.

After a couple of months, I went to visit him. We had a really good time talking. He had two adult daughters by that time and caught me up on what had transpired since we'd last seen each other in 2001. I stayed there for a few hours then had to leave to pick up my kids. He asked me to come back the next day if I could. I left work a little early the next day and called to let him know I'd stop by. He asked me to stop and get him a Red Bull because he worked third shift. I stopped at the store that one of my other ex's ran to get it. He was giving me attitude and asking why I was buying a Red Bull. I told him I was thirsty but he knew I didn't drink them and insisted I tell him what dude I was getting it for. I ignored him and headed to the house.

While driving, my head started hurting. I didn't want to disappoint him so I went on to see him. When I got there, we sat at the table and chatted until I laid my head down. He looked around the kitchen for something I could take and found a pack of pain pills. I took two and he told me to lay down so they could help before I had to leave. Normally I am pretty perceptive and take time to look around when I visit men at their homes. This time I didn't though because I didn't feel good. I hadn't talked about him to anyone so I couldn't ask about his dealings. It felt friendly enough that I didn't need to do my usual "check" to verify what he'd told me. And in typical "keep your ass at home" fashion, I'd regret that as well.

That day, briefly, we ended up intimately involved. Please know that when I say *brief*, trust me. Blink of an eye type encounter…

When I left, I knew I wouldn't return. I felt bad that I even let it go there. I was extremely worried thinking about how long it had been since I'd seen him. I had no idea who or what he had been into. I worried that I could have contracted something for having unprotected intercourse, however brief. I went through the typical prayers and bargaining with God that we often do after we've put our big girl panties on. I stopped communicating with him as much and tried to get back into my routine.

Janea went to stay with my mother due to increasing issues at home. My mother only took her in to disagree with me. I had to pay her to keep her and after she kept demanding more money outside of the agreed upon amounts, we talked about Janea leaving her place. By the time Janea was ready to graduate high school, she was tired of her grandmother and whatever she was being exposed to there. She was staying at a classmate's house practically every night to avoid the shenanigans at her grandmother's house.

When the poop hit the fan and grandma clocked out, I sent my younger sister with Janea to get her things. My sister waited outside while Janea went inside. I guess my mom came out behind her cursing and threatening her. My sister tried to intervene to keep her from hurting Janea and they ended up in a physical altercation. It was ugly. I was so upset when I received the call. I couldn't believe this was happening. My mother blamed me for the incident and told people I sent my little sister over there to fight her. That was absurd! I was the only child she had who never disrespected her, hit her, nor took from her. I was so confused as to how I always became the villain even when I was nowhere near the scene!

Janea stayed with her aunt until she got ready to go to college. My sister filed charges against our mother for the attack and they had to have an order issued to stay away from each other. This was all too familiar as my mother and older sister had the same thing happen to them some eight years earlier when my older sister attacked my mom's friend and tried to fight my mother. Those were exactly the reasons why I tried to keep my distance from her when she got in that nasty combative mode. She normalized abnormal behavior and then complained about not having a relationship with her kids.

IRISH TWINS
2011-2012

The night of the big fight, I had some friends over and we were preparing to go to a party. The fight caused a great deal of upset, but I made sure both my sister and daughter were safe before being convinced to go on to the party and try to have a good time.

I went and did have a good time. I wasn't able to finish my drink because I wasn't feeling well and was extremely tired. My friends chalked it up to the stress of the earlier events in the evening. We went to get food and then headed back home.

As the days passed, I was increasingly more tired and then I missed my next period. I attributed that to stress as well and continued with my day to day living. After the second missed period, my friend started ribbing me because we came on at the same time and she warned me not to visit Speedy. She joked and told me I would get pregnant if he spit on me. I hadn't intended on being intimate anyway so I paid her no mind. Finally, I broke on down and took the pregnancy test. Oddly enough, I didn't see it coming because I was more worried about an STD than a baby! But just like that, with a toddler turning two soon, I discovered I was pregnant yet again.

It was just too much! All those years I dealt with Speedy when I was young and vibrant and not once did I get pregnant. I could not believe it! If you think I had a hard time, the reaction from him was really wild. He was in total denial and did not believe I was pregnant at all. I hadn't seen him in a couple of months. He had been asking me to come back over but I refused. When I told him about the baby, he said he wanted to see for himself. I refused and tried to move on with the issue of what to do with a whole baby on the way. He goes right into the "I didn't get you pregnant" line. That sent me into attack mode. Understandably enough, we both had been away from each other for a while but in the talks we'd shared, I told him I had been single for years and celibate since the pregnancy in 2009. He continued to stand by "not getting me pregnant" even though he did not use protection nor ask if I had any.

After months of the back and forth, I left it alone and started to find a way to reconcile the fact that I would have an infant and toddler very soon. This pregnancy put me in the "advanced maternal age" category. I had to have blood drawn more frequently and see the doctor more often. When I got the first ultrasound and found out it was a boy, I sent it to his address with a letter to clear the air. I didn't wish to be with him romantically but hoped to find a common ground of which we could build a relationship to co-parent the child.

He called me with a story about his "ex" coming by to see him as the mailman delivered the letter. She opened it and came in questioning him about the ultrasound. He called himself warning me because she was planning to call to ask me about it. I assured him she would get no information from me. He obviously lied to me and was living in her house when he invited me over. That was reprehensible! I was angry. I would never enter another woman's home to be with her man (using the term very loosely). Our son would be his first son so I thought the call would be more of his excitement than the nonsense he called about. After that, we couldn't find common ground. He insisted I was not pregnant by him and he would need a paternity test. Apparently, he had not been following along and missed the memo that paternity tests were my new normal. We ended up getting the test which came back 99.999999996% positive.

It was still eighteen months before he would physically meet his son, Jaeon, a quiet and wise baby. When they met, they spent very little time together. Here and there but Speedy's life was in turmoil and I respected him for protecting our son from that.

Meanwhile, George was experiencing child support issues—he didn't want to pay me! He wasn't fond of any of the kids I had after his and rebelled by neglecting his own. We stayed engaged in a war over money. I wasn't financially pressed but angry he had the money, flaunted it, and refused to do his part. The twins were starting to rebel and yearning to be with their father more. He wasn't having it. He lived with a younger girl and her two kids near our home. We'd see him out riding with them and it was upsetting for us all.

George never really got over me walking away as I told him I would one day. He wasn't used to women telling him how it was going to be. He was the only boy growing up and spoiled by the women around him. I had no intention nor desire to continue that pattern. Everything he did to hurt his kids was out of spite. He was seeking a way to hurt me the way my leaving hurt him. The next year would begin a battle that took more out of me than I desired but I would learn so much from it as time went on.

IF YOU LOVE THEM, SET THEM FREE
2013-2014

My twins started sneaking out to meet their father without my permission during Spring 2013. He refused to have any communication with me when I tried to set up a schedule for them to visit with him. I asked that they come home from school and keep me informed of their whereabouts. Janea was secretly encouraging them to do what their father said and aiding him in attacks against my character. Being that she always sought his love and approval, she was often used as the mule to interrupt harmony in my house.

By this time, she came out as transgender and identified as male. She lived independently and was struggling to find her identity. My heart broke for her because she endured so much pain as a child and was still suffering within herself. She was not able to accept her beauty and many people tortured her for it. We supported her in the transition but not in the disruptive behaviors she exhibited along the way.

After many times of the twins disobeying me and a decline in their school work, I put them on punishment. The older twin was withdrawing and staying in a dark room every day. I began to really worry about him and his patterns. He refused to open up to any of us. I asked if he wanted to go stay with his godmother for a while and he said no. This was cause for alarm because that usually represented a safe place for him to take a break. I then asked if he wanted me to call and see about him possibly going to the hospital for an evaluation. He said yes and that tore me up. He had never agreed to go.

I got his things together and we went to the hospital. We had done this before when he refused to follow rules in the house but whenever we'd go there, he would get it together and they'd send him home. This time, they recommended he stay for inpatient treatment. He told them he was okay with that as well. I cried like a baby when I left him there. I could feel something truly different taking place but trusted that God would see us through.

I chose not to let his siblings know what was going on because I knew their dad would intervene and block his treatment. Oddly enough, while in treatment, he signed an affidavit to have his father kept away from him. To this day, I have no idea what that was all about. The doctor told me he had a fantasy of who his dad was and needed to come to grips with the fact that he may never be that man.

My good friend saw my daughter on the bus and asked how her brother was doing. She assumed she knew about him. As expected, she told her father what was going on. He showed up at the hospital belligerent and demanding to see him. They called me in a panic and asked what to do. I advised them to have security put him out! What were they calling me for? Policy is policy! He threatened to have his lawyer come to the hospital. Just being an ass.

He called me and asked for the code they gave me to see him. I tried to explain, to no avail, that the code was only for me and he was not allowed to have any visitors until they finished evaluating him. He cursed me, threatened me, and continued to verbally harass the staff at the hospital.

My son called that night and said he didn't wish to see him but he looked forward to my upcoming visit. I was scheduled to see him and meet with the doctor a few days later. On the day I arrived, I was pulled into a room and told I would not be able to see him. The doctor told me an order had been sent over by the court giving their dad custodial rights. I could not believe my ears nor my eyes once she showed me the order. Apparently, his lawyer filed a motion for emergency custody. A court date was set and they never served me with the papers. Because I missed the court date, they gave custody to their dad. Low down and scandalous!

I immediately broke down. The doctor told me they would try their best to restrict him based on the affidavit my son signed. I was dizzy, nauseous, and heartbroken. All I wanted at this point was for my son to be okay. I called my mother to tell her what happened. She was sympathetic and said she'd pray for me. She was talking to Nate on the phone before I called and said he wanted me to call him. I did and he soothed me a little. He told me to calm down and think about what I needed to do to make this right. He offered money if I needed it for a lawyer.

Regina called next saying she'd heard about the custody. I was leery in speaking to her because my spirit told me she would immediately connect this to me "taking her kids" which I never did but I listened to her anyway. She said she was sorry that happened but started talking about "when her kids got taken away" and I just held the phone. I had no time for this right now. I assured her the ruling would be reversed and ended the conversation.

I spoke with my biological father and he was very supportive. He scolded George for being so petty and vindictive and offered to call some people he knew. I thanked him and told him I'd keep him posted. When I called Mick, he was sorry and sad. He told me to keep him posted and assured me everything would work out.

When I got home, the other twin was there. I was clueless as to why he would be home if the court took my custody. Turns out, George just wanted the son he favored. I immediately called the courts to let them know that he filed papers erroneously accusing me of being dangerous and unfit yet left a whole kid with me who he was granted custody of. The next day, he was forced to pick the other twin up from school. He also picked up the twin from the hospital. My heart ached because I was not able to see him and hadn't since I dropped him off. It would be six weeks before I'd see my son again. They switched the custody back within three days but the twins were with their dad at that point so I decided to leave them until the court date. He did not take them to the house he lived in with his girlfriend and her kids but instead sent them to his mother's house. I hoped they could see through this behavior and know he was not acting in their best interest.

No go! When the court date came, they walked into the courthouse and refused to speak to me when they came in. It was two days after my birthday and none of them said a word. On that day, I learned my daughter had gone to her dad's lawyer and told him lies about me abusing them. I could not believe it! The very person who had inflicted so much pain on her and who I fought tooth and nail not to do so, paid her to corrupt our home! She proudly stood with him as he planned to uproot her brother's wellbeing.

My lawyer came and let me know the judge was disgusted with the presentation their dad gave and he was clearly not fit to raise a dog. He did say my kids spoke against me and stood by what he had to say. When the judge asked where they wanted to be, they chose him. The lawyer cautioned that keeping fifteen-year-olds somewhere they didn't want to be was bad and could destroy my family. I told him it had already started. They were being mean and abusive to my younger three kids and I'd never seen that before.

I had to make the decision right then and there to do what was best for them all. I agreed to let them remain with their dad. I told the lawyer George had them at his mother's house instead of his own and wasn't keeping their medical appointments. The older twin had a heart condition that required monitoring and the younger twin was in treatment for emotional conditions. They ordered him to keep them in school in our county and keep all of their appointments. I asked for visitation every Wednesday so they could attend Bible Study with us and every other weekend. I knew it would be bad having them going from house to house too much. They had proven it was very different in the households when they visited with him years ago. They came home with attitudes and acted out. Being older now, "acting out" took on a whole different meaning.

Their dad sent messages taunting me about taking my kids and gloated that he'd won. It was very exhausting. My younger kids cried because they didn't understand their brothers being taken away. Pepe was still with his wife but remained supportive. He was having some legal issues and not around physically. Speedy was also going in and out of jail during that time.

It was more than enough to deal with and I started to break. The first scheduled visit we had did not happen. When I tried to call to see what was going on, I was hung up on. I couldn't believe the boys would not at least call to let me know they weren't coming. When I called the school, I learned that their dad moved the younger twin from his school. I had them in separate schools because Eugene suffered from identity issues of the younger twin. He thrived when he wasn't in Jaree's shadow. This was upsetting. I called Jaree's school and found out Eugene had been moved there. They told me they couldn't tell me anything else because I was not listed as a contact for either child. George took the old custody order that was only valid for three days to the school and had me blocked! I could not believe after being the only parent involved all of their lives, I suddenly couldn't get any information. These people knew me but swore they could not "bend" the rules for me!

Eugene had been in fights at the new school and even had charges taken out on him after being robbed by bullies. The doctors were calling me asking why they hadn't been brought to their appointments. This was spinning out of control! I called child protective services at the request of the doctors to ensure he upheld the order and got them to their appointments. I also filed a motion about my visits being taken. The twins went before the judge and refused the visits. I knew then that I had to make a choice. I knew how heinous their dad could be and wanted no harm to come to them. It became crystal clear that in order to be with him, they would have to be without me!

A week later, I ended up in the emergency room with elevated blood pressure that almost caused me to have a stroke. I had to be put on blood pressure medicine. Over the next six months, I existed without my oldest three kids. My daughter was doing interviews with the local news media about being homeless since she was a child and making up stories of us having no money. My heart ached for her because she was having a mental breakdown right before our eyes but would not accept the help she needed. My mother called and asked for money to pay her bills and lashed out when I refused to give it to her. Regina had moved to another state but continued to wreak havoc when she could.

During the summer of 2014, I went to the store to pick up my medicine. I heard someone calling my name as I got in my car. When I looked back, it was Nate and my mother. I was so happy to see him! He told me she was helping him pay his bills and find an apartment. He told me he loved me, was proud of me, and would call me later. When he called, he said he had broken up with his girlfriend and was ready to step out on faith to change his life. I told him I would help however I could.

When he got his apartment, he came over to pick up some things I had for him. He came in and we talked for a long time. He assured me that my boys would always love me and would return. We talked about my mother briefly. He said he knew he needed to stay away from her because her spirit wasn't right for him. She had been talking down to him about me and he didn't like it. He couldn't understand how she wasn't happy to have me as a daughter and proud of my accomplishments. I told him I was okay and continued to live my life regardless. He discussed some things about his relationship with his own kids that hurt him. Then I comforted him by telling him it would all work out. We went into the backyard and he played with the little guys. He told them he planned to come around more so they could get to know him better. We loaded up his car and he went to get in. I noticed he was moving rather slowly and seemed to be in pain more than usual. We said our goodbyes and I love yous.

A few days later, I got a call from my mother ranting and raving about what I said to Nate about her. I was pissed because I couldn't figure out how we went from him being tired of her to this! I let her know it wasn't that kind of discussion and got off the phone. I decided not to call him with it but I was disappointed in him. When he called, I saw his number and did not answer. I didn't feel like listening to it that day. After the mess with George, I was really trying to limit my intake of other people's bull!

Nate left a message asking me to call him but of course I did not. The next week, August 1, 2014, as I'm sitting on the toilet, I get a text from my mother that reads, "You know Nate's dead." I looked at it and blew it off because I called him Nathan and who would think a mother would text her daughter something like that about the one man who stood in as a father unconditionally? I figured it was someone from the streets and could not care less. I called her when I finished and asked who the text was about. She said she guesses Nathan is dead because that's what someone just called her and said.

My heart dropped and I immediately got off the phone with her and called my uncle who was his sponsor in Narcotics Anonymous. My uncle said he hadn't heard anything about it but talked to him before he left town for the weekend. I called his phone and wasn't able to reach him. My uncle said he called someone and they said Nathan had missed the meeting that day. I told him I would meet him at Nate's place and proceeded to get dressed. My stomach was in knots as I made the twenty-minute drive to his place in about twelve minutes. I kept trying his phone and got nothing.

As luck would have it, I got there first. I knocked on the door and no one answered. I saw his car so I truly believed he was going to open the door. While knocking, a neighbor opened her window and asked if she could help me. I told her I was looking for my father. She asked if it was Nate and I told her yes. She said she was sorry to have to tell me that Nate passed away. I broke down on the sidewalk. She told me she hadn't been outside due to an illness so she couldn't come to me. I appreciated her consoling words. I felt so alone and distraught. She told me the police came by to do a welfare check and found him inside. He body had already been removed.

I called my mother and uncle screaming. They were on the way. Oddly enough, my mother was just a few blocks away and should've been there before me. She was the last one to get there. My uncle's girlfriend, Kim, came to my car to sit with me. I helped Nate's children make arrangements for him and stayed by their side throughout the transition. It was so hard to let him go but I had to accept that he was not well and deserved peace.

We all came together to celebrate his life. Mick always felt some kind of way about my relationship with Nate, so he wasn't very supportive during my grief. He was still wrestling with my biological father being in my life as well. Ray was an avid reader of the newspaper so he saw the obituary for Nate and asked about him. I explained who he was to me and he offered his condolences. It was very genuine and I appreciated it.

CELEBRATIONS, GRADUATIONS, SALUTATIONS
2015-2016

Shortly thereafter, I finished my second masters with a degree in School Guidance Counseling. I learned my little sister was pregnant with her second child and she'd been struggling recently with her stability. The news was hard to digest but I gave it to God because I knew this would be the time for her to grow up and deal with the choices she made.

The pattern of babies after deaths missed me this time. I hadn't dated anyone since 2009 and hadn't been intimate with anyone since Jaeon was conceived in 2011. That one did it for me! She could go right on and have that tradition.

In March 2015, my fourth niece, Addy, was born. She was a precious little light! My really good sister-friend, Tori, was expecting as well and gave birth to her daughter two weeks later. Her sister, Nikki, had a baby boy in July. We were being blessed with these bundles of joy to make things brighter.

The twins were allowed to visit here and there with little to no conflict. During their visits, I learned how bad it had been for them. They were shown folded papers and told my family signed saying we wanted nothing to do with them. They were berated by George's girlfriend and forbidden to speak to any of us when they saw us out.

One day, there was a school shooting at their school. I rushed over when I heard about it. We were all in a panic because the media said a fifteen-year-old had been shot but there were no other details. I, of course, didn't even know my sons' phone number to call. When I called George's job, he gave me nothing. I tried to call his mother and she was very evasive. She was watching it on the news from her house but no word on the boys. My aunt lived closer to the school than me so she got there first. They interviewed her on the news and she cried when talking about how much she worried about the twins and loved them. Once I got there, we had to just stand back and wait for them to release the students from the building.

When they started walking the students out, I saw my twins coming out. I was so happy! Luckily, there was a member of my church who allowed me to get inside the area they were in to speak to them. My aunt saw them before I did and they were unusually cold towards her. She asked if someone had told them not to speak to her and said one of them told her he loved her but could not say. When I got to them, she was crying and walked away. I tried to hug Eugene and he snatched away. When I went to hug Jaree as I cried, he pushed past me and said he was okay. I decided not to make a scene and went back to my truck. I cried huge heaving sobs. I wasn't even able to rejoice with my sons that they were okay. I later learned that the dad's girlfriend was there and she was reporting back to him so they couldn't speak. His mother also alerted him that I was there. He was not.

I saw the boys several more times and received the same thing from Eugene each time. He was mean and refused to communicate at all. This was hard being that he was my baby boy and thrived off of contact. He seemed afraid. My mother told me God had told her the twins could be in danger. She feared someone would hurt them if we continued to pursue contact. I prayed on it and resolved to let it go. I had male friends who encouraged me saying all boys return to their mothers. They knew how much I loved them and how good I was to them so they were confident that no matter what they were being told, they would find their way back home.

I ran into Lando and he was very helpful in keeping my spirits up. Although he reminisced about days of old, I kept it strictly platonic with him and enjoyed talking to the older version of the teen I once knew.

As 2016 began, the twins were slowly coming into their independence and deciding they wanted to be around their family. Things were tense where they lived and they yearned for the familiarity they once had. They started to sneak and call more. I kept having dreams of making peace with George so I reached out to him. I asked if he could let the boys call me once in a while and if we could see them. He shortly replied that they could call if they wanted to and no one was stopping them and hung up. So much for my dreams.

When prom season came, I wasn't able to see them get dressed or have any contact with them. A few weeks prior, it was Derby weekend here. The twins were downtown at the Chow Wagon, a festival where different vendors sell food and apparel, and various concerts take place. Khy asked if he could go meet them. I wasn't sure how that would work but the boys called and said it would be okay for me to drop him off. When I took him, we waited at the corner for them to arrive. When I looked out the window, there stood Jaree over six feet tall. I could not believe my eyes! I jumped out and gave him a hug. I was lifted off my feet in doing so. I don't know what they were eating, but he was not that tall when I saw him last. Tears of joy filled my eyes. I was so overwhelmed. Their friends were there so Eugene tried to play it cool. This time he did hug me though. I could barely contain myself. Khe and Jaeon jumped out to hug their brothers. We had to cut our reunion short though so I could get to the fireworks show we were attending. I told them to call me when they wanted me to pick Khy back up.

As I was leaving, I saw their dad riding by in his car. My stomach was in knots and something told me there was more to come! I called the boys and let them know he was in the area. We went on to our destination. It wasn't too long before Khy was calling and saying I needed to come back because someone called their daddy and told them he was with the twins. I tried to call my friend to see if she was nearby to get Khy in case I wasn't able to make it in time. Eugene was nervous but he stayed and waited with Khy until I got there. I was livid that their daddy demanded them to go home and leave Khy there. He had no threshold for how low he would go.

I didn't see or hear from them for a while. I wasn't able to participate in their prom festivities and had to find pictures on social media. They looked so handsome though. I wasn't given information about their graduation either. I went online and found everything I needed and even sent announcements out to my family and friends. Those ceremonies are very public and I would not be denied that joy. I had other relatives who were graduating from the same school so we sat with them.

When the graduates began to come out, I went down to the ropes to see the twins come through the walkway. When Jaree saw me, he smiled. Poor Eugene, he smiled but the look turned to sheer terror when he looked over and saw his daddy standing on the opposite side. It was so unfair. He couldn't even be happy to see his mother on his special day! I went back to my seat and tried not to let it kill my vibe.

I wasn't able to get to them after the ceremony due to the large crowds. However, my aunts were and I learned later that it wasn't good. While visiting with them in the back of the auditorium, there were some words exchanged between my aunt and their grandmother and dad. They gave them their gifts and left. Because of whatever had transpired, they weren't allowed to come to my house that evening. Two weeks passed before they made it.

I kept their gifts and also had three years' worth of Christmas, Valentine's, and birthday gifts to give them. They opened everything but I noticed that they were not taking their cards and anything big. When I asked why, they told me that any gifts they received from my family were thrown away. Their dad would have them open them all in front of people and then make them throw the gifts away. My family was crushed. I hurt so bad for them to have to go through that. We enjoyed the time we had them with us and I encouraged them to hang in there. They assured me they would stay in touch.

Time went on and we kept in contact as theseasons changed from summer to fall. Regina was back in town and found yet another reason to be at odds with me. These incidents were beginning to be frequent and out of order. Our mother would either provoke her or ignore her. I lost count and increasingly wanted nothing to do with either of them.

In November 2016, I received a call from my good friend that my nephew, Shawn, had fallen down and sustained a very serious injury. He is Regina's oldest son and my whole heart. I left work and rushed to the hospital. My mother came and we waited to hear what happened. When Regina got there, I acted as if nothing had gone on and consoled her when she almost passed out with grief over her son's condition. He had fallen and was unconscious. He suffered traumatic brain injury and it looked bad for a minute. I stayed by my sister's side throughout the dark days and nights and attempted to reconcile whatever the issue was that time.

We kept in touch over the next month as my nephew recuperated. I went to his home, brought groceries, and helped with paperwork he needed done as he healed. I picked my sister up, loaned her money, and helped buy Christmas gifts for her kids and grandkids. Friends of mine helped with Christmas for her grandson. All was well as long as I was giving.

SHIT HIT THE FAN
2016

As I was leaving to meet a parent who wanted to help with the Christmas gifts, I noticed a nasty smell. My younger sister called and told me that my mother had been to my house earlier that day. I told her I must not have been home because I didn't see her. She said mama saw my truck in the driveway. I thought about it and recalled that I had been in my basement cleaning up. I assumed that was when she came by and I didn't know she was there. I didn't see any missed calls from her phone though. My sister said she was mad saying I knew she was outside and didn't let her in so she shit in my yard. We both laughed as I was loading my truck. I brushed it off as nutty and kept it moving.

When I stepped on my porch to get another load of gifts, I realized the smell was following me. I looked down right as I stepped into my doorway and screamed! There was a hunk of brown on my boot. I looked at the porch and steps and saw more of the brown. You could've sold me for a penny right then! I realized that I had been walking in poop. It was in the grass right outside of my passenger side door of the truck. I could not believe my eyes. My sister was still on the phone and responded, "Well, she did say she had to shit."

The next few moments were surreal. I began to seriously look back on the many heinous things my mother had done to me over my life and this incident was a defining moment for me. Yes, she has bowel issues. Yes, she may have really had to go. But no, not in my yard. It hurt me to my core that she would do that, leave it there, and not even consider the fact that I have small boys who play in the yard! They could've stepped in it. Her action was cold and heartless. I believe she really thought I was in the house watching her knock and simply refused to let her in. But that was not the case at all. I would've did it in my car before I subjected my kids and grandkids to that! I felt that she metaphorically considered herself "shitting on me." It was the ultimate disrespect as far as I was concerned. This is my home that I worked hard to own. Her good friend lived on the next street. She could've driven there or shit in the next yard!

Anywhere but in mine.

When I got to Regina's house, she pulled up. Regina tried to help move her away from my window. She got out being confrontational like always when I told her I didn't want to hear it. She continued to tell me I knew she was out there and totally ignored the fact that she disrespected my home. Regina consoled me and told her to go home. She said she couldn't believe that happened and mama should've at least let me know it was there and tried to clean it up.

By now, most relatives chose not to get involved when she did those kinds of things but they supported me. I told my dad (Mick) and he laughed. That was his typical reaction to things they did to me. He said he couldn't understand why she did that and left it there. When I told my biological father, he was livid! He wanted her number to call right then and there. He went back to the anger he had for her keeping the secret most of my life. I told him to leave it alone. I was used to being mistreated and this too would pass.

I refused to speak to her. As if it wasn't enough, I keep my garbage cans in the driveway of my home. About a week later after a storm, I found a napkin in the driveway with poop on it. I thought about it and it occurred to me that the napkin was further evidence of the heinous part of it all. Even after the rain, it was still there for me to see that she wiped and threw it on the ground. She could've put it in one of the three cans but chose not to. Somewhere in her mind, she wanted me to know. Well, she did tell my sister. We just didn't take it seriously because, who does that? Thank God the year was ending! I had experienced more than my share of foolery and was definitely ready to move on. We celebrated Christmas and believe it or not, I sent my mother Christmas and birthday gifts. I try to honor my parents regardless of how they parent.

THIS YEAR I RESOLVE TO
2017

January brought a wonderful event to my life that could potentially right all wrongs! New Edition was celebrating their movie coming to BET and being given a star on the Hollywood Walk of Fame. Being a part of the NE for Life universe, I was elated when my sista-friend said we were going to go. I got my plane ticket, a sitter, and made arrangements for the trip. I hadn't been to LA since I was a pre-teen so it was long overdue.

The week we were scheduled to leave, Eugene called me at work and said he couldn't take it at his dad's house anymore and was ready to go. They were back at their grandmother's house during the week to attend college and went to his place on the weekends. At some point, George married the girlfriend and her behavior got worse. She complained about Eugene's diagnosis of Asperger's because she knew nothing about it and instead of educating herself, she chose to nitpick his issues. His dad physically got on him whenever he lashed out at her in frustration. I was upset and called a friend who lived in the same city as his grandmother to bring him home. His twin drove so he told him he would get him to my house. I didn't like the sound of that at all but he wanted to trust his brother.

Come to find out, his twin drove him to Louisville and took him straight to their daddy. He gave him grief about wanting to come back home and told him he was cutting him off. It got much worse but for the sake of preserving the peace we've obtained the past year, I'll skip it.

When I got home from work, his dad's truck was in front of my house. His twin was removing bags and sitting them on my porch. He didn't even speak to me as I got out of my truck. I asked what was going on and nobody answered. Eugene was standing on the porch with tears in his eyes. I went to George's window to ask him if he was okay with the transition. He rolled the window up and told me he wasn't talking to me because I'm always getting stuff started. I hadn't spoken to him in years and was hella confused as to why he was acting like that. I was proud of myself for calmly saying anything after all the hell I'd endured at his expense!

He continued to rattle on about nothing as Jaree put the last bag on the porch and got in with him. I asked Jaree why he took his brother to him to be mistreated and he just looked out the other window. I lost my cool and started yelling. Got in my truck and backed into the garbage cans trying to get back on the street. I realized my little guys were in the car and they wanted to know why I was crying. I had to regroup fast. It was clear God had sent those two last babies as a calming force for me. I wiped my face and went in to see how Eugene was doing. He was hurt and upset. I know how much he loves his brother and did not want to live separate from him but it was apparent that he was choosing to remain with his father. We didn't hold it against him.

By choosing to come to me, Eugene lost his phone, games, and bank account. I wanted him to be clear that as his mother, I would never let him do without. Within the week he had a new phone, bank account, and a car! We made sure he had a fresh start with love. While I went to LA, my oldest came to stay with the boys. I left my vehicle and money for them to be entertained. We had the time of our lives in Los Angeles including attending a live taping of Jimmy Kimmel's show and the ceremony at the Walk of

Fame, and eating at Sweetie Pie's NOHO (for me cause I was a diehard fan of Miss Robbie) and Roscoe's Chicken and Waffles.

Being a gameshow fanatic, I wanted to find a few but no one else was interested. On Sunday we visited Warryn and Erica Campbell's church, Cali House of Worship. It was such a wonderful experience. I've been a fan for many years and prayed to attend the service and meet them if possible. I was able to meet Erica and Tina after the service. My heart was full!

I returned home and got back to my life. Eugene was doing well with us. He was happy to be back and even managed to connect with his brother. He started receiving flack for coming over but by now, had grown tired of having to sneak around. He asserted himself and let his dad know he loved us and would not be kept away. That made me happy.

Unfortunately, we were on the outs with my oldest due to a breakup she had. She got angry at us for remaining friends with her partner. She'd legally changed her name and gender. She didn't tell me directly but took it upon herself to talk to her younger brother about it and tell him he couldn't refer to her as female any longer. I was angry about that because I'm his mother and she should've spoken to me first. I tried to have a conversation with her about things her ex brought to my attention and she became irate. She yelled and said I never supported her or took her side. This was blow up number 9999 or so. Always the same thing—correct something she does wrong and bloop! Never did anything for her, don't love her, don't support her, should've aborted her, the foolery goes on and on! It becomes crystal clear that between my mother, sister, and her daddy talking bad about me to her most of her life, she's going to continue to spout nonsense when she can't have her way. I grew tired of her behavior, so her tantrums grew numbered. Maybe everybody was just on one for 2017. I started the year off resolving to cut out the drama though so every time somebody tried to bring me the smoke, I shut it down expeditiously! Miss me with it.

That summer, my sista Shaun and I planned a trip to Jamaica. She was a frequent flyer but it would be my first time flying internationally. The trip was well-earned. I had grown tired of the dysfunctional relationships with the people I called parents. My mother was still in timeout for the poop, my daddy stayed away until he needed something, and the biological got an attitude because he kept trying to get me to visit him alone to "get to know me better" and I couldn't make that sound or feel right. I don't know how much better he thought he could know me without my kids being there. No deal, whatever the case!

I kept in contact with my sister Rey and even found out that a really good friend of mine from high school was the father of my niece from another sister I met. Unfortunately, the sister who'd gone to my church passed away from an illness. I never got to meet her and was saddened to learn she had three small girls. I did try to reach out to her mother to meet the girls but was never contacted.

Pepe had gotten himself together to some degree and was helping out a great deal with the boys. He was very fond of Jaeon even though he wasn't his father. He agreed to keep the boys when I went to Jamaica and they were excited to stay with him.

I'd started using Instagram and actually met a cute guy on there. We messaged quite often and I was enjoying his company. While in Jamaica, he sent me a message saying he was stranded in Malaysia or somewhere and his credit cards were stolen. He's the manger of his own oil rig company but has no way to get back home to his ten-year-old daughter, to which he is a single parent.

Shaun was humorously intrigued and told me to offer help just to see what he would say. I wrote back and told him that although I was a single mother with limited resources, I would help however I could because I'd never want to see a child without her father (which was true). I guess he had a pang of guilt. He told me I was so sweet and thanked me but did not send an amount. I knew he was a scammer though because the picture of him was this bright handsome man with a buff bod, yet all of his followers were older women who were not the most attractive or presentable. I think he was a gigolo scamming lonely women for money.

Over time, I would meet a few more of his same type. I just pray one of them really wasn't a wealthy oil miner sent to save me! After his bull, the minute they said oil, engineer, or overseas, I chucked the deuces!

Shaun and I continued to enjoy the last few days of our trip and when it was time to go, I watched Shaun's heart break. She probably could do good just renting herself a place there. She was in her natural habitat when she visited Jamaica.

I met a handsome man at a restaurant the night before we were scheduled to leave. He flirted throughout dinner and before we left to attend a show, he asked me to come back before the bar closed. After we left the show, I stopped back in to see him as they began to close. He may have been the manager because he gave orders to the staff as they cleaned up. He was really intense as he spoke to me and asked if I could meet him when he closed the place. I told him I needed to check with my friend and didn't want to leave her alone. Of course, when I went back and told her, she thought that was the best thing ever! He had plans for me and my trip would end on a happy note she said. I begged to differ! What about me winding up chopped up in a bag?!? I was homesick and ready to go! A rendezvous in the back of a closed restaurant didn't seem conducive to my plans to get back home to my family. No, not even a little bit.

As luck would have it, our layover in New York was delayed and we had to stay overnight. I was not trying to hear that so we looked for a rental car to drive home. Unfortunately, it would cost us an arm and leg so Shaun, who was much calmer than I was, convinced me to stay. I called Pepe to make sure he was good with watching the boys another day or two. He said it was okay but I wasn't convinced because most of the times I called, they were not available to talk and when they were, Khe looked sad and filled with angst so I knew there was more to the story.

We called hotels to find none were available in New York. Thus, began our bootleg escapade to New

Jersey! I kid you not, I can't make this stuff up. We called the hotel from the airport and they booked our stay. We only needed one night and found the basic amenities in their ad plus, the price wasn't too bad. By the time we got our rental car, we were exhausted. We mapped the hotel and ended up in a rat-infested parking lot that touched the projects. I was sure we were in the wrong place. The building looked like the building from Good Times and there actually was a huge rat waiting at the door with his bags!

I assured Shaun I would not be going inside and called to ask for a refund. They had already taken out the full fee and said there were no refunds. I was fit to be tied! I let the seat back and told her I would sleep in the car. Me and the rat would not be checking in together.

Against my better judgment, we went inside. The lobby had a big area with the front desk enclosed in bullet proof glass. I told Shaun we probably needed to sleep back there or go back out to the car. They had all of these ridiculous hand-written signs that further confirmed we needed to sleep in the car. Dumb stuff like, "Bottled water $3," "WIFI available but only if you leave your driver's license at the desk," and many other signs. I was now sleepy and cranky so I needed to get checked in and away from the madness as quickly as possible.

We walked down a dusty, musty hallway looking for the elevator. I suggested we head right on back out the door we came in but Shaun laughed and reminded me it would only be for one night. She made the grim error of asking how much worse could it be. Stay tuned…it got better!

We got to the room and opened the door to find two twin beds, a tiny bathroom, and a closet. I couldn't believe it. Was someone renting out apartment rooms or were we paying to sleep at the mission? Needless to say, we were there for the night and starving. We went to the store to get some things and ventured through the city looking for food. By then, it was late and dark so we settled on a chicken joint.

I was a nervous wreck as we waited forever to get our food. Shaun has the patience of a saint and was content while we inhaled a mix of marijuana and gun smoke. Praise be to God we were able to get our food and make it back to the hotel without incident. I refused to use the bathroom and wrapped myself in a sheet set I always carry when I travel. I dozed off after eating while Shaun took a bath, got comfy, and slept like a baby in her twin cot.

The next morning, we woke up early and set out

to explore Jersey before heading to New York to catch our flight. We didn't have a great deal of time but wanted to visit the cemetery where Whitney Houston and Bobbi Kris were laid to rest. We had no idea what we were walking into and really just came up with the idea as we got dressed. The graveyard was easy enough to find but we had no idea where the actual burial spot was located. It's a large cemetery so we had a lot of ground to cover.

My investigative skills are on point so it didn't take us long to figure out which part of the cemetery housed the more affluent graves. We also looked it up on Google maps and tried to relate where we were to the pictures. However, after awhile, we realized we were being followed. We stopped when we saw it was a police officer and asked if he could point us in the direction of the graves. Bad idea. He told us we needed to leave and that the graves were in a private site.

Well, us both being math teachers, and I, a special education teacher also, could not quite digress how the cemetery is public as hell but he's standing here telling us that we need to leave. Bad idea flashlight cop! Shaun is sweet but not when you cross her. She asked him what we were both thinking almost verbatim to how I worded it and he got angry. Told us he would call the Jersey PD to lock us up. We found considerable humor in that statement and laughed in his face. We'll wait for you to call back-up for two tourists here to grave dig and steal treasures from Whitney Houston's tomb.

We'll wait…

He went on to tell us how the Houston estate paid him to watch it because people had burglarized it before. Okay Robocop, shouldn't you be by the grave and not here talking to us then? What's left? Did they put more jewelry in there after it had been burglarized once? You'll have to excuse me cause I'm highly analytical.

Shaun was pissed and being the ex-wife of a police officer, had her feeling herself. I thought it was quite notable to mention but reminded her we were in Jersey and it probably wouldn't do us a lick of good if they knew once we were arrested. We told him we would leave and did no such thing. We continued to drive and tried to get a glimpse. We'd likely not get back to those parts anytime soon! He followed us a bit and after he turned his lights and siren on, we admitted defeat and headed to breakfast.

After breakfast, we went to downtown New York so I could buy some souvenirs. Shaun is a road rage driver so after maneuvering through the city and about 500 expletives, she decided not to get out. She circled the block while I shopped. Once I was done, we took the car back to the car rental place and prepared to fly back home.

The boys were so happy to see me and I was ecstatic to be back home. Pepe was on edge and in a rush when he picked us up from the airport. I noticed Khe was very quiet and his daddy yelled at him when he tried to talk to me. We took Shaun home and headed to my house. He unloaded the truck and barely took the things in before he was gone. He was barely out of the driveway before Khe let loose the juice! He said his daddy had left them at his "friend's" house and the friend yelled at him because her son couldn't play with his toys. I asked him why he wasn't at the house his daddy lived in and if his daddy stayed where he was. He said his daddy didn't sleep there but him and Jaeon did. I had never met this person and knew nothing about her. That posed a big problem for me. I texted Pepe and asked him about the arrangements. He immediately got defensive and said the female he let keep them was his "sis" and they stayed there because she has a small son and they wanted to play. Suspect. He never mentioned anything about the girlfriend he was living with at the time. Never met her either but I knew of her, and they had taken the kids a couple of places.

I'd left my house keys with him and told him he could stay at the house with them and have Khy watch them if he needed to go out. Khy told me his dad told him he could stay at his friend's house when I wanted him back home. Khy felt bad that he didn't persist and his brothers were uncomfortable where they were. I was furious with Pepe because my mother left me with strangers as a kid and I longed to be back home. I never wanted my kids to feel that. He jumped on the defense because he knew he was wrong and from that point, our co-parenting relationship would never be the same.

IF IT ISN'T LOVE
2017

As fall settled in, people around me talked more and more about the dating site, Plenty of Fish. I entertained the thought of an account but quickly dismissed it. I didn't want to mess around and end up on a missing person's commercial just trying to find companionship.

My sista Shaun and I were hanging out and going to different events around the city. While shopping at the outlet mall on September 11, 2017, I saw Chico Bean walking down the sidewalk. I was excited to see him because me and my boys were obsessed with Wild 'N Out and knew them from the show. He stopped and took a picture with me. I didn't know they were in town for a show and when I heard about it, I got a ticket and planned to go. My little brother John agreed to accompany me to the show. I got dressed and met him there. The show was off to a great start. We had a drink on the way in and the hilarious Carlous Miller opened the show. I was excited for DC to come on because I could relate to his humor. He came out and immediately started ripping the people coming in late. There was a guy with one of those rolling walkers. He let him have it and I almost wet my pants. After that, he told a joke about his friend's disabled sister and being left alone with her. If memory serves me correctly, the joke ended with him having sex with her. I laughed so hard I had tears coming out and a little urine. As DC left the stage and intermission started, John told me he was going out to get more drinks. Since I had to use the bathroom, we both headed for the hall.

All I remember is walking down a few steps and then hearing noise. I realized someone had fallen and heard people asking if she was okay. I must've blacked out because I suddenly was in the air and then hitting the floor. I landed on my feet and kind of rolled over when I hit the floor. I quickly jumped up and grabbed my new designer handbag from the floor. I still had to use the bathroom and although I was slightly dazed, I proceeded to get there.

People walked right on past me and could not care less that I had just fallen. The usher, a Black older man, saw me fall and everything and never even asked if I was okay. I asked where the bathroom was and he pointed towards a long hallway. I started headed in that direction and noticed with each step, how much the pain increased. At one point, I fell against the wall and found a drunk guy leaning alongside me. He looked and kept going as if to say, *she's drunk like me*. I winced in pain but knew I needed to make it to the bathroom.

When I reached the end of the hallway and went inside, a few ladies were already standing around outside of the stalls. I leaned on the sink in pain while waiting for a stall to come available. When I finally got in a stall, my eyes started to water and I could hardly stand. Being a germaphobe presented an entirely different set of problems. I couldn't dare let my body touch the toilet. As I squatted to use it and used my legs to balance, I cried out in pain. It was then that I told myself my ankles were broken. I can be dramatic at times, but I was pretty sure this was the real thing. I managed to finish up and get to the sink to wash my hands.

By now, the bathroom was empty. I pulled out my phone and texted to let my friends and family know what happened. When I called John, he thought I was joking. I wasn't in the main bathroom and really couldn't explain to him where I was. When

I got back to the usher, a nice lady approached me and asked if I was okay. All the pride and ego in the world immediately left my body and I told her no! I was in so much pain, it was hard to breathe. She had me walk up what had to be about fifteen steps to let someone else know I was the lady who fell. They took me to the lobby and called the ambulance. All the cool completely left the building! My ankles hurt like hell! The pain was much worse than any of the labors I'd experienced. I waited in agony for the ambulance to arrive. John found me and like a true ride-or-die, tried to give me the drink he had been holding for me. If only I'd known how long I would sit in the ER, I would've enjoyed that drink!

I waited for over five hours to be seen by someone in the ER. I kept in contact with my kids so they knew what was going on. Eugene was at the house with Khy and the littles were with my aunt. Janea and Jaree stayed on call in case they were needed. My mother was still estranged at the time. I called my daddy and he said he hoped I would be okay and to call back. I called my biological dad and he was very alarmed. He offered to find someone to bring him to the hospital but I told him not to come. I was in so much pain, I didn't want to have to entertain anyone.

After the third hour, my phone died so I took a

moment to reflect. There were sick people all around me. I had my face covered because a flu outbreak had started. The pain got so bad, I cried. Once I read, pain can be so bad, it makes you have a stroke. I took a moment to talk to God. I had been through some tense moments throughout my life and asked that He give me strength to make it through this too. I focused on getting home to those boys who graced my life with their unexpected presence. I was seen, given X-rays, and told my ankles were indeed broken. In the excitement of the day, I never even realized it was 9/11 when I broke my ankles! I had to have surgery the next week and a screw put in my left foot. I stayed off work and began to heal.

I purchased a trip to the Bahamas for my birthday weekend to see New Edition perform. I had almost a month to get myself together. Unfortunately, it didn't happen. It wasn't wise to go that far from home without being completely healed. I stayed home and set up my account on Plenty of fish (POF). I saw a few good-looking guys but no one interesting.

I got a ticket to a comedy show after my birthday where a funny comedian who told teacher jokes would be in town. I texted my friend, Netta, to see if she wanted to go. She replied and said no because her aunt only had a little time left and she wanted to be with her before she transitioned. My heart dropped. Netta and I met in high school. She would always go on and on about her aunt. One day she showed me some pictures and I told her that her aunt looked familiar to me. When I kept thinking about the photo, I realized her aunt was my head start teacher. I found the school picture and took it to her the next day. She couldn't believe it. I reached out to her aunt and from that day, she became a strong presence in my life. She ran a daycare that many people in the city patronized. Over the course of our relationship, she'd had every one of my children at some point in their lives. She was a very wise woman and we grew very close after the twins left. She prayed with me, encouraged me, and spoke candidly to me as a divorced mother. She'd been fighting cancer heroically for the past couple of years. I thought she was doing better so the news hit really hard.

Within the week, she was gone. My heart was broken. My youngest said he needed to send her a card because she was the best teacher he'd ever had. I thank God I was able to send her a text the month before letting her know. She often told me it was time for me to find a man to love. I told her I'd pass but she could find her a man to love. She laughed and told me she was good on that. I said, me too, and she said she's old but I'm still young. Often, I dismissed those words but now my heart was aching, my feet were aching, and I had plenty of time on my hands.

The night she passed, I got a message from a good-looking man named Mark on POF. He started off like everyone else saying hello and telling me how beautiful my pictures were. I was sad and really not in the mood but something told me to respond. He had good conversations and we talked into the wee hours of the morning. Before we hung up, he asked if he could have my number and I gave it to him. It would turn into the first relationship I'd had in more than ten years. We spent time together while I was off work. In November, Shaun and I took a trip to Atlanta to attend Ronnie Devoe's (her mental husband) 50th birthday party. We had VIP tickets and had a ball. I actually found myself missing him while I was away. He was very calming for me and a fun guy to be around. We had a lot in common. We were both divorced, raising sons, and disabled. It was ironic that my accident somewhat led us to connect. I knew God had to be doing something in my life because I was humbled after my fall. Watching Mark do so many things in his condition was amazing. He said I brought new things to his life and he experienced the truly giving side of a relationship. He took me on trips, bought me gifts, and even hung out with my family. He encouraged me to make things right with my mother, if at all possible, and I told him I'd do what I could. He was from the same area my dad lived in when I was younger so they had similar accents. He was loving like all of the dads I'd experienced growing up and I enjoyed being with him.

But as 2018 began, the sunshine turned to rain. He had a problem with my relationship with Pepe. It was practically non-existent due to him dating a much younger woman who was not happy about our friendship. He kept her away from me but wanted to have her be in the mother role to appease her. When he realized I was seriously dating someone, he went all the way left. Stopped coming to get his boys and totally shut Jaeon down. Wouldn't even speak to him at times.

I was walking in my new life with less drama so I didn't entertain it. I'd given George too many years of foolery so I had no more to spare. Mark became insecure and started to cramp my style. His attitude changed and I noticed he was okay with the strife occurring with my kids and their father but kept his kids safe from any discomfort of us dating. We argued more. I was fine with that because I felt nothing should be rosy all the time. He believed people shouldn't argue or have disagreements.

In January 2018, Shaun lost her father. It was hard to hear her say those words through the phone. She had a bond with her daddy like nothing I'd ever seen before. My heart broke for her. When I told Mark what happened, he was nonchalant. He had previously said he didn't feel there was any need for people to cry about traumatic events. It would still be the same when you finished crying. That threw me for a loop.

I made plans to fly to Virginia to be with her when her father was laid to rest. He didn't care for that. I make rash decisions when I'm grieving so he was walking right off the plank. The morning I was due to fly out to meet her, I received a call that my beloved Pastor Walker had succumbed to illness. I was caught off guard and in a tailspin. He had been an important part of my life since I was ten years old. I couldn't see through the tears. I canceled my flight and tried to find my way through back-to-back tragedies.

I was actually in a good place with Regina, my mother, and my dad but had not spoken to my biological father in about a year. I took his daughter and her new baby in the year before. She was ungrateful and took advantage of my home and kindness so she left abruptly. I guess he was in his feelings about her leaving (although they were on the outs when she came to live with me) and opted not to return my calls. Janea had been staying with mom at the time. All of my children were distraught about Pastor. It was so unexpected and we weren't able to see him due to his illness. He had a very big celebration of life the following week and I had to watch it from home. It was tough to attend the wake so I knew not to attend the funeral in person. I cried and cried and tried to believe that God had a bigger plan for his life while also worrying about my sista who was overcome with grief as well.

Two weeks after Pastor's funeral, Janea calls and says that the man in the store they go to told my mother that no one had seen Ray in five or six days. I didn't know what they wanted me to do because as I said, I hadn't spoken to any of them in over a year. She said she would go by his place to check on him. My aunt called me and said she heard people were looking for him too. Not real sure why, but she went to his house and banged on the door. I told her I had already heard from my mom and Janea. With everything I was going through, I didn't want to get mixed up in it. I was having headaches and my blood pressure had spiked sending me to the ER.

A woman from my church who had a daughter by him as well told my aunt they found him dead in his home. After another week, I get a message from Rey saying they needed money to bury him. I was stunned. The nerve of people! Not one of them reached out to me when he was missing or when they first found him, but here she comes looking for money. I was cordial though and told her to check on his veteran status and see what they could do. The only other correspondence I got from her was a post about his funeral. I had already decided I would not attend. Something in my spirit said it was time to let it go.

I only sought him out to know who I was and to be sure there were no health issues of which I needed to be aware. He had over fifteen kids all over the place and there was no way I would ever know them all. No one did and he would not answer any inquiries about his kids with a straight answer.

In the end, I mailed a check to his brother to help out because he'd attended my graduation and sent me one Christmas gift. I sent that amount to help. When I called to check on his brother, they addressed me as Ms. Dixon (from the check) and had no idea who I was. When I told him my first name, he immediately recalled who I was. His daughter was appalled. She shared with me that she'd asked the five children of his who went to the funeral home with her if there were any other siblings to name in the obituary and they said no. She forgot about her father mentioning me years earlier.

The truly ornery part is that they all knew about me long before I ever met any of them. He went on about me my whole life. They were just nasty and spiteful. I was told other sisters were mad at me because I looked more like him than they did. I knew I would not dare take on that foolishness after all I had already endured in my own family. Plus, I had my own daddy so the struggle was not the same for me. His niece apologized for the oversight and said she was going to say something to them for doing that. I told her his daughter, Rey, lived with me. I took her in when no-one else would. The other sister came to my house to help her move out. One of them knew me since I was young and kept telling people I was her sister. In the wake of all that ugliness, I was sure I would not attend any services. There had been enough pain and I was just ready to breathe again.

Apparently at some point after the poop incident, Ray saw my mother in the store. She approached him trying to "tell" on me for not giving her my number. He blasted her about what she did. She called and told someone else I got her cursed out. She was livid saying he never did nothing for me and had no right to be talking shit to her. She walked right into it. How dare you try to make me look bad to someone you deliberately kept out of my life!

That being said, she was in a better place and very happy with my decision not to go. However, a really good friend of mine couldn't seem to get on board with my decision. She kept pressuring me to go. I tried to let her know it was not in alignment with my healing process. She persisted and ended up getting unfriended in real life. She was someone I'd been friends with for almost thirty years but had to disconnect from often. My other friends and family always said she was jealous but I gave her the benefit of the doubt. She lost that when the argument went from me going to a funeral to the fathers of my children. I really didn't know how or why the channel changed, but I was no longer subscribing to the network. Ironically enough, I often said my new boo, Mark, was like the male version of her. By then, I was done with both of them and chose March 2019 to sign off!

GRACE AND MERCY COVERED ME
2019

Janea decided to attend the service and was angered by the lack of interaction she received from her aunts. I told her to let it go and keep it moving. My dad really surprised me when he called to give his condolences and asked how I was doing. We had a long talk that day and he truly seemed like a weight had been lifted from his shoulders. My mother too. I wished it was under better circumstances but I was ready to move on.

I thought about the Father's Day ritual I had grown used to once I found out. I had to strategize who was going to get their gifts dropped off first. Ray wasn't jealous where my daddy was concerned because he knew he raised me in his absence. But my daddy was so bothered by my interactions with Ray, it was always a potential disaster.

After reconnecting with him and knowing his

health was failing, I tried my best to keep the waters calm. However, Father's Day 2017 pushed me to the limit. It was raining and I always made sure to honor my uncles because they were the most consistent fathers I had. It had been a long day trying to get them their gifts. I was on my way to drop off something to Ray but remembered that if I went to his house and then to my daddy's, the little ones might say where we'd been and ruin the day. They had no idea what was going on and I would never censor them. It was raining hard and I ended up having to get my dad's gifts to him before it got too late. He lives near my house so I had to go back the other way more than ten miles to Ray's house. My resilience was waning, and I longed for peace. Him making the call that day seemed to be it.

In March a close friend whom I'd recently met teaching invited me to come to her church for Women's Day. She was young but very spiritual. We said we had been placed into each other's lives for a divine purpose. I started going to Bible study with her and Sunday service. I could feel my life doing something special. I was keeping in contact with my mother, my daughter, and even my sister who was back in another state. My twins were in a good place with their daddy. He started to move away from the negative and they were able to co-exist with both of us. I truly felt so much better having dissolved the relationships that were not purposeful. I was eating better and really moving closer to God and His plan for my life. I joined her church Easter Sunday 2019.

That May, during a routine mammogram that I'd been getting since I was nineteen, I found out I had Stage 3 breast cancer. I had to have a biopsy done and actually heard God speak to me when it was done as I waited for the blood to stop. I heard him say, "It's okay. You did it!" I laughed and cried simultaneously.

During that same time, my mother fell and hurt herself. She broke her leg and had to be put in a nursing home for rehab. When I called to tell people about the cancer, the only times I cried was when I told my mother and my older sister. My mother assured me right away I would beat it because she did and I was strong like her. I felt so good. Regina started off very supportive and sent positive words often as I went through my surgeries. It didn't last long though. It almost seemed as if her mood changed when I beat the cancer. Her words became cruel and hurtful and I decided I wanted to stay well and could not let anyone get in the way.

Eugene moved in with my dad and they seemed to be getting along well. Everyone grew a little closer in the wake of my diagnosis and truly tried to stay close and love one another…

IF I COULD
Summer 2020

We have been living through a pandemic and sheltering in place for several months. I've spoken to my mother several times, sent texts, and even went to her house to take her some custom masks I made for her.

When I saw her in April, she didn't look like herself at all. She'd mentioned some weight gain but I wasn't at all prepared for what I saw. She was dark, her stomach was huge, and she looked like she had been blown up with an air pump. She told me she was in a lot of pain but she said that often so it didn't cause any suspicion. I called my dad as I drove away wishing I'd taken a picture of her. I also told my aunt and sister what I saw. It was weird.

I sent her a package for Mother's Day and called to verbally express my love as well. She wished me a Happy Mother's Day and said she knew I'd have a good one. I didn't hear from her anymore until the Sunday before Memorial Day. I sent her a Happy Memorial Day text to which she responded, "same to you."

Monday, June 1, 2020, I received a call from my aunt telling me another sister was at mom's house waiting for the police to come to do a welfare check because no one had heard from her in seven days. She didn't want them to call me right away due to my high blood pressure and anxiety issues. I immediately walked back to my room to take my meds and a nerve pill. I told her I wasn't going to go down there but to keep me informed. I had a sudden urge to use the bathroom and it happened three times back to back.

On the third time, God's voice told me to get down there. I got dressed and called my younger sister as I headed downtown. I talked to my dad's mother as I drove to get my sister. She spoke nice words about my mother and tried to assure me everything would be okay. My stomach was in knots as I drove. I learned that Regina started calling from Georgia when she wasn't able to get mama on the phone. One of her sisters in Georgia was also concerned. Although neither of them had reached out to me leading up to this day nor on the day. At this point, I believe it was deliberate not to let me know as they assumed my mother and I were estranged and did not deal with each other. It was not the truth. We had actually gotten along fairly well after I was diagnosed with breast cancer. She was a champion in my fight and recovery. She encouraged me to stay strong and told me I would beat it just like she did. It was so! I had spoken to her by phone and/or text consistently since January of 2020. I guess it's much easier for hateful people to ASSume the worst than pray that old wounds are healed and hearts are reconciled. I know God took us through the journey of healing together to make our Earthly goodbye bearable and I thank Him so much for that!

As I got closer, I could see several police cars ahead and people out in the front yard. My uncle called right as I pulled up and told me she was in the apartment. I breathed a sigh of relief. But then he said that she was gone. I asked what he meant and he said she was dead. I parked my truck and got out to see my aunt crying. They said the police officer had already gone in and identified her and no one else could go in until the coroner came. I started crying and could not process what I heard. We dreaded this day but knew sooner or later it would become a reality.

I got myself together so I could call Mainty and tell her. I called my adult children as well to let them know. Janea was there waiting in the hall and had to be subdued because she wanted to get into the apartment. My oldest son came from his job and consoled me. His twin was coming over from Indiana. We waited outside the door in agony of what we would find on the other side of the door.

I left and went to pick up Mainty who has always been my rock so she could be there with us. Several other family members were on their way as well and when I returned, the coroner had already been inside. He had me sign something and told me I could call a funeral home to come get her body. I called the funeral home Nate worked for when I was a teenager and asked them to handle her arrangements. They told me someone would be by shortly and the coroner let us in the apartment.

My mother was in her bed. We took some time to say goodbye and tried to figure out what happened. I believe she passed in her sleep. I'm not sure how long we were there with her before the funeral home came but it seemed like forever. I sang her a song when I had a moment to be with her by myself. Regina Belle's *If I Could*. I used to sing it for my daughter. She carries so much pain and heartache in her life and I just wish there was a way I could take the pain. In that moment, I felt the same thing for my mother.

I was recently contemplating how birth order and being born into a large family could really be a burden to some children. My mother went through so much throughout her life but she could mask the pain and still have the most beautiful smile anyone had ever seen. The black Cher is what some people called her. She could light up a room and partied with some of the best!

I was left to take care of everything. I began going through her things as we waited for Regina to get to Kentucky. She wanted to be cremated and have her ashes scattered where my twin girls were buried. She always called them Itsy and Icey for some odd reason. Never called them Jameah and Jamae. That was mama though—her way or no way!

While reading through mounds of paperwork, I noticed she would write on any and everything. Sticky notes, envelopes, in books as she read, etc. Oddly enough, I do that too. She wrote by my name that I didn't love her. On an envelope from a letter I sent her in 2013, she wrote that I didn't love her, never wanted to see her again, and would not help her. I had to actually take the letter out and read it. There was nothing in the letter that said that. She turned the words around and made them suit her agenda.

When speaking to a couple of her friends that

week, I learned that she referred to my conception as rape. She had never revealed that much detail to me but it made sense. She told a friend the incident is what led her to start doing drugs. I was now presented with a window into her soul. She never bonded with me when I was born and had been saying that to me most of my life. Whenever I would ask questions about my birth and infancy she would say I needed to ask my daddy because she didn't do nothing but push me out. I found out at sixteen that my middle name was wrong. She simply said, "I don't know. Ask your daddy, he named you!"

Now I could see why she was so disturbed when I met my biological father and began to develop a relationship with him. She felt betrayed that I could be close to him when he had violated her. Neither of them shared that part with me but I knew some of the story. I felt bad for her. As a woman, I can identify with being forced into situations and having to present a totally different scenario to others. I'm much more vocal and was never able to keep secrets. There is definitely a liberation that comes with being able to use your voice and speak your truth. Unfortunately, many victims are not able to do so and live haunted by things they were never able to cry out about.

I always felt she was jealous of me and my success.

I wondered how she could have three daughters and complain so much about the two who gave her the most grief yet treat me and my kids so unkind when I strived to do well and not be an issue to her. She loved my kids but they could feel the disdain she had for me. She talked about me to them and that put a strain on how they felt about her. They opted not to be around her much, as did I. She put so much space between me and Regina that my sister took on the jealousy and hatred mama often exhibited. They would double team me and unleash a fury like nobody's business.

Before my grandmother died, she sadly told me she had never seen a mother and daughter behave that way. She couldn't understand how the two closest women to me treated me the worse. That being said, she also told me you have to love people not like them and that they did not need to be in your life if they didn't know how to behave. That was priceless advice she gave me the week she died. I coined the phrase, "You will respect my presence or feel my absence" and haven't strayed from it. I don't care who you are, the message is the same.

* * *

As I finished cleaning my mother's apartment after a week of tirelessly doing so with three of my aunts, one of her neighbors came out to say goodbye. She told me she was proud of me for doing what my mother expected me to do. She knew Regina was long gone back to her home and my younger sister was home as well. She laughed and said, "Sherie knew who would get it done. She always said you were her responsible child. You were the one who would make sure she was alright!"

I stood frozen for a minute, allowing it to marinate. It was refreshing because when she had an accidental overdose scare a few years back, both times I was called and had to handle everything. I prayed at that time for God to give my mother peace however she needed to receive it. Even if He had to take her from this world I would be alright with it. No one should have to walk this Earth for so long in so much pain. I envisioned in my mind back then that I would have to pay to put her away and started saving money to do so. Now here we were during a pandemic and that dream was now a reality. I went to the funeral home and wrote a check for her cremation.

The finality of it all hit me hard. I have bargained with God before so I knew better than to even act like I had a problem. He has never let me down and can do anything but fail! I thanked Him for her life—good, bad, or indifferent. She was my mother. She loved me to the best of her ability and fought the demons until the day she died. I remember her saying, "I did the best I could and we don't get a handbook on how to be a mother when we have kids." Amen to that! She was a force like no other and left a myriad of people who loved her. She fought for those she loved and would give the shirt off of her back to those in need. Her life was not in vain and we will celebrate her transition. She rests now and we have another day to get it right.

My maternal grandmother, mother, biological father, and Nate are all gone now. They all died in their homes alone while someone stood on the other side of the door wondering what was going on. I'm not sure what the connection is, but I received a wealth of love from them all. My father Mick is still here with me. I picked him up on the Saturday before Father's Day and shared with him what I'd found. He was shocked to hear the rape part. I told him most women abort or give the baby away when they are put in that situation. He told me that she wouldn't have had those options because he thought the baby was his. That made sense and opened that window to her soul once more. He has since brought up the wounds he hasn't healed where the biological father is concerned at the hands of Regina and I choose not to be held in that bondage any longer so that relationship has been severed. My mother lived in agony through a pregnancy she didn't want, a marriage she was not happy in, and kept the secret of what happened to her while she visited Louisville one weekend. She went back to Texas with nothing but fear, shame, and despair.

Bless her soul. It is well now, and I am walking in the light that has surrounded me from day one. I was not meant to carry the burden of knowing those harsh details any time prior to right now. God's timing is so perfect! He is always on the throne! I am living my life today in alignment with what God has for me and I AM NOT MY CONCEPTION!

"I finally understand for a woman it ain't easy!"
- Tupac

www.ingramcontent.com/pod-product-compliance
Lightning Source LLC
Chambersburg PA
CBHW060356080526
44583CB00012B/332